Assessing the Economic Impacts of Environmental Policies

EVIDENCE FROM A DECADE OF OECD RESEARCH

OECD
BETTER POLICIES FOR BETTER LIVES

Please cite this publication as:
OECD (2021), *Assessing the Economic Impacts of Environmental Policies: Evidence from a Decade of OECD Research*, OECD Publishing, Paris, *https://doi.org/10.1787/bf2fb156-en*.

ISBN 978-92-64-82482-9 (print)
ISBN 978-92-64-36711-1 (pdf)

Photo credits: Cover © Krunja/Shutterstock.com.

Corrigenda to publications may be found on line at: *www.oecd.org/about/publishing/corrigenda.htm*.

Foreword

Policy makers have long been conscious of the consequences of environmental degradation and the COVID-19 pandemic has further raised and renewed awareness of the inherent fragilities of our environment. Yet, their ambition to address environmental challenges such as climate change, pollution and biodiversity loss has often been held back by the perceived immediate costs of more stringent environmental policies on people and firms. Businesses and policy makers alike fear that differences in the stringency of environmental policies across countries would negatively affect the competitiveness of firms located in the most ambitious regions. Pollution-intensive production would shift towards countries or regions with less stringent regulations, altering the location of industrial production and the subsequent international trade and investment flows – and potentially curbing the environmental gains. These fears are particularly apparent in the case of climate change mitigation, where a large gap exists between globally stated ambitions – as laid out in the 2015 Paris Agreement – and the climate policies actually adopted around the world.

This report brings together unique analysis that sheds light on the above issues. It presents evidence from a decade of empirical research by the OECD on the impacts of environmental policies on firm performance, productivity, employment, trade and investment across countries. It provides novel insights for policy makers about the costs and benefits of environmental policies, both at the aggregate and micro levels.

Our analysis shows that implementing more stringent environmental policies has so far had little effect on overall economic performance, despite achieving clear environmental benefits. However, there are unavoidable localised impacts that can generate winners and losers across firms, industries and regions. To ensure a socially inclusive transition to a greener, low-carbon economy, it is critical to recognise the costs for some, and provide appropriate policy responses to mitigate these costs: environmental policies must be combined with policies that support negatively affected workers and facilitate the transformation of industries and regions. This can help cushion the adverse distributional effects, strengthen political support for these policies, and raise and widen ownership of the goal to tackle climate change.

The recovery from the pandemic provides a unique opportunity for governments to "build back better" and to steer the economy onto a trajectory of greener growth. Over 120 countries have already committed themselves to achieving carbon neutrality around the mid-21st century, but achieving such targets will require significantly more ambitious climate policies and transformative change in many economic activities. With all eyes now on COP26 in Glasgow this year, we encourage governments to look at this report for direction and support to reinforce their commitments and climate policy actions.

Laurence Boone
OECD Chief Economist and G20 Finance Deputy

Rodolfo Lacy
Director, OECD Environment Directorate

Acknowledgements

This publication is a joint output of the OECD Economic Policy Committee, the OECD Environment Policy Committee and the OECD Committee on Industry, Innovation and Entrepreneurship.

This volume was edited by Antoine Dechezleprêtre from the OECD Directorate for Science, Technology and Innovation and Tobias Kruse from the OECD Economics Department and Environment Directorate, under the overall responsibility of Shardul Agrawala, Head of the Environment and Economy Integration Division in the OECD Environment Directorate, Giuseppe Nicoletti, Head of the Structural Policy Analysis Division in the OECD Economics Department, Peter Hoeller, Head of the Public Economics Division in the OECD Economics Department, and Chiara Criscuolo, Head of the Productivity, Innovation and Entrepreneurship Division in the OECD Directorate for Science, Technology and Innovation.

All chapters were authored by Antoine Dechezleprêtre, Tobias Kruse and Vera Zipperer from the German Institute for Economic Research (DIW).

Chapters 2 to 9 were initially prepared by Vera Zipperer and were reviewed by the authors of the working papers underlying each chapter. Thanks go to Silvia Albrizio (Bank of Spain), Arlan Brucal (University of Exeter), Damien Dussaux (OECD), Grégoire Garsous (OECD), Daniel Nachtigall (OECD), Balazs Stadler (OECD), Dennis Dlugosch (OECD), Frank Venmans (LSE), and Christina von Rueden (OECD).

The authors would like to thank Nils Axel Braathen and Walid Oueslati from the OECD Environment Directorate and Alain de Serres and Tomasz Koźluk of the OECD Economics Department for excellent comments and suggestions on an earlier version of the manuscript, as well as delegates to the OECD Working Party on Integrating Environmental and Economic Policies (WPIEEP) of the Environment Directorate and of the Working Party 1 of the Economics Department for useful comments and suggestions on the working papers underlying each chapter.

Table of contents

Tables

Figures

Boxes

Follow OECD Publications on:

http://twitter.com/OECD_Pubs

http://www.facebook.com/OECDPublications

http://www.linkedin.com/groups/OECD-Publications-4645871

http://www.youtube.com/oecdilibrary

OECD Alerts http://www.oecd.org/oecddirect/

Executive Summary

Governments have gradually adopted more stringent environmental policies to tackle challenges associated with rising environmental issues, such as climate change, air pollution, waste management or biodiversity loss. Between 1995 and 2015, the stringency of environmental policies related to air pollution, energy and climate change – as measured by a composite indicator developed by the OECD – tripled across OECD countries.

The ambition of these policies is, however, often shaped by their perceived negative effects on the economy. Indeed, environmental regulations generally require polluting facilities to undertake abatement activities, which imposes costs on businesses. Therefore, policy makers fear that, in a world characterised by the rise in global value chains and capital flows, differences in the stringency of environmental policies across countries would change relative production costs and alter firms' competitiveness. As a result, pollution-intensive production capacity could shift towards regions with less stringent regulation. This would modify the spatial distribution of industrial production, with potential consequences for employment, international trade and investment flows.

However, the results of a decade of ex-post OECD studies on the economic effects of environmental policies on industry, summarised in this publication, show that implementing more stringent environmental policies has had little aggregate effect on economic performance so far despite achieving significant environmental benefits. This publication summarises eight recent OECD studies investigating the link between environmental policies and economic outcomes, based on cross-country firm-level, sectoral and macro datasets. The studies reviewed in this book find that:

- Short-term effects of environmental policies on aggregate economic outcomes have been modest so far. A 10% increase in energy prices generates a decrease in manufacturing employment of less than 1%, a small increase of around 1.5% in foreign investment relative to total investment, no net effect on trade, and a slight increase in productivity. Across all of these outcomes, the impact of environmental policies is overwhelmingly dominated by other determinants of economic performance and other public policies (trade policy, labour market policies, factor endowments). However, more work is needed to understand the longer term effects of environmental policies.
- At the same time, environmental policies implemented in the past had significant benefits in terms of environmental outcomes. For example, the introduction of the European Union Emissions Trading System led to a reduction of carbon emissions of 10% between 2005 and 2012. The French carbon tax reduced emissions by 5% between 2013 and 2018. The removal of energy subsidies in Indonesia led to declines in energy use and carbon intensity (of respectively 5% and 10%, for a 10% increase in energy prices). In all of these studies which assess the impact of environmental policies on environmental and economic performance jointly, the effect on employment and other measures of firm performance were either insignificant or very small.
- However, these small average effects across the economy hide heterogeneous effects across sectors and firms. On the one hand, environmental policies adversely affect the performance of mainly high-pollution industries (e.g. manufacturing of petrochemicals, iron and steel, etc.) and of least-productive firms. Specifically, employment, exports and investment are negatively affected

for pollution-intensive companies, as is the productivity of firms that are initially less productive. On the other hand, more stringent environmental policies also have positive effects, like improving productivity of front-runner industries and firms or increasing exports of low-pollution industries. Overall, environmental policies generate winners and losers and trigger a reallocation of capital and labour from high-emission to low-emission industries and firms.

- The design of environmental policies matters and can help mitigate the negative impacts and enhance the positive effects. For example, using market-based policies rather than command-and-control policies is found to help offsetting negative productivity effects.

Despite their small adverse effects on the economy, implementation of stringent environmental policies remains politically difficult because the localised effects can be large (e.g. in terms of employment or competitiveness losses), even if small overall, which can generate strong opposition. Therefore, from an efficiency, distributional and political standpoint, it is important to design environmental policies in a way that emphasises their positive net effects for the economy without sacrificing their impact on the environment, while also helping those individuals working in the most polluting companies.

In this respect, an advantage of market-based policies is that they generate additional public revenues. These can be used to address potential adverse distributional impacts of environmental policies, to fund environmental innovation and investments, to reduce the tax burden elsewhere in the economy, or to reduce public deficits. Nevertheless, market-based policies can be administratively more demanding to implement because of monitoring requirements, and can also be socially less acceptable.

Combining environmental policies with other policies (such as trade, education, employment and fiscal policies) can also play an important role to deal with the challenges associated with the unavoidable negative effects of environmental policies on the least-efficient, most polluting companies. For example, active labour market policies (such as facilitating job search, enhancing skills, life-long training and education) – especially if enacted early – can ease the transition to a cleaner economy.

A note of caution remains: The studies reviewed in this publication make use of historical changes in the stringency of environmental regulation, largely related to energy, air pollution and climate policies, to analyse their effects on economic outcomes along various dimensions. While this provides valuable lessons, future increases in environmental policy stringency made necessary recently by adopted carbon neutrality targets may lie outside of observed past changes. Low-hanging fruits of energy savings and resource reallocation might have already been exploited, and further emission reductions might require radical technology changes and vast resource reallocations. If such radical changes were necessary, the conclusions drawn from the studies might not be generally valid, particularly in a world where countries implement climate change policies at a different pace. Continued empirical evaluation of environmental policies will be necessary to allow governments to fine-tune policies and balance environmental goals with impacts on economic performance of industry.

1 The economic impacts of environmental policies: Key findings and policy implications

This chapter summarises the conclusions from the report and presents the main policy implications of these findings. It shows that environmental policies have become more stringent in OECD countries over the past decades, but at a different pace across countries. The empirical evidence in this volume shows that climate policies have been effective at reducing emissions from industry. At the same time, the policies had relatively small effects on economic outcomes such as employment, investment and productivity. The evidence suggests that well-designed environmental policies do not have large negative effects on the economy. The policies can however generate winners and losers. Policy packaging can help compensate workers and industries that may lose and strengthen public support for more ambitious environmental policies.

Introduction

The world is facing increasing environmental pressures in numerous domains. These include rising air and water pollution, climate change, biodiversity loss and waste generation. At the same time the COVID-19 pandemic has triggered an unprecedented health crisis resulting in a sudden economic downturn. Post-crisis economic recovery programmes provide an opportunity to "build back better", and to align economic recovery with climate objectives (Box 1.1) and (OECD, 2020[1]; OECD, 2020[2]). The growing awareness of the urgency of a structural transformation of the global economy has brought environmental policies to the forefront of national and international politics in the past decade. This is illustrated by numerous initiatives such as the Sustainable Development Goals (SDGs), the Paris Agreement on Climate Change, or the European Union's Green Deal. Between 1995 and 2015 – the period which studies summarised in this book focus on – the stringency of environmental policies related to air pollution, energy and carbon emissions, as measured by a composite indicator developed by the OECD,[1] increased significantly across OECD countries (Figure 1.1). Average industry energy prices[2] – which are affected by energy taxes, carbon pricing and other environmental policy instruments to reduce pollution associated with fossil fuel energy consumption – also increased substantially (+50%).[3] What has been the impact of these increasingly stricter policies on the environmental and economic performance of firms in the manufacturing sector? This book offers an overview of empirical OECD work from the past decade on this question.[4]

Box 1.1. Environmental policies and the COVID-19 pandemic.

The COVID-19 pandemic poses a major challenge to economies and societies across the world and it might weigh on economic policies over several years (OECD, 2020[3]).

Economic recovery programmes present an opportunity for governments to 'build back better' and to warrant that efforts of meeting climate objectives are not derailed by the pandemic. Well-designed environmental policies can play an important role in aligning the recovery with climate objectives to limit warming to well below 2°C, in line with the Paris Agreement. Learning from previous crises when designing green recovery packages can help ensure more effective policy design (Agrawala, Dussaux and Monti, 2020[4]; OECD, 2020[1]; OECD, 2020[2]).

To meet the targets of the Paris Agreement, a first priority is to avoid the weakening of environmental policies. Investments in energy technologies require long-term planning and policy certainty. Weakening environmental policies increases uncertainty that can delay or discourage investments (OECD, 2020[1]).

Green stimulus packages can help strengthen economic growth and support investments in green technologies (e.g. renewable energy, battery technologies, etc.). Nevertheless, green stimulus packages and investment support for green technologies are not sufficient to deliver continued investment in low-carbon technologies. Longer-term signals are necessary. The removal of fossil fuel subsidies and clear commitment to carbon pricing trajectories can help align price signals, and make investments into climate mitigation technologies more viable.

The studies reviewed in this book provide support for the effectiveness of environmental policies in reducing emissions. Moreover, they show that environmental policies have little aggregate effect on economic outcomes of firms. Well-designed environmental policies – specifically market-based approaches – are suitable and required to help governments align the economic recovery with climate objectives to limit global warming to well below 2°C.

Figure 1.1. Environmental Policy Stringency and energy prices, 1995-2015

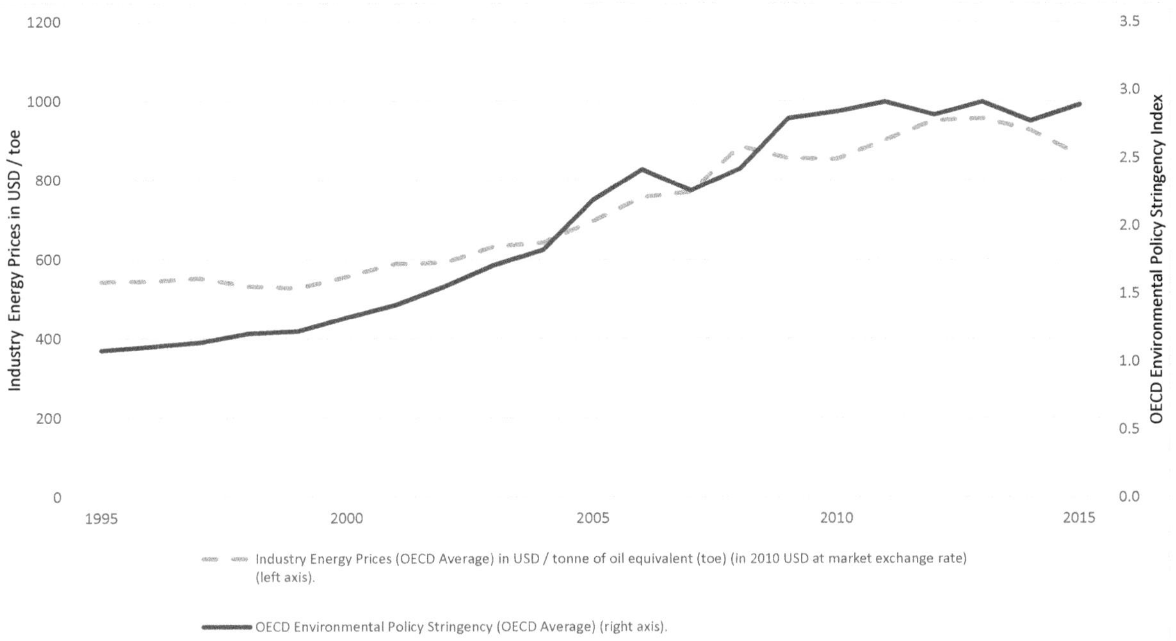

Note: The figure shows the OECD Environmental Policy Stringency (EPS) indicator for the OECD average (solid line, right axis) and industrial energy prices (dashed line, left axis). The OECD EPS average is an unweighted average across 28 OECD countries for which data are available. The industry energy price data are taken from Sato et al. (2019[5]). The values are computed from their VEPL_MER variable (Variable weights Energy Price Level at Market Exchange Rate). It is based on a weighted average of fuel consumption by fuel mix. The graph is based on their industry-level prices which covers 12 industrial sectors across 25 OECD countries.
Source: OECD; Sato et al. (2019[5]).

Environmental policies and competitiveness concerns

Over the two decades that preceded the Paris Agreement, environmental policy has become more stringent at a different pace across countries. Figure 1.2 presents the level of environmental policy stringency across OECD countries in the years 2015 and 1995. It shows significant heterogeneity in the environmental policy stringency across countries, including between countries of similar level of economic development. Some countries also ramped up ambition stronger than others.

Figure 1.2. Environmental Policy Stringency Indicator across countries

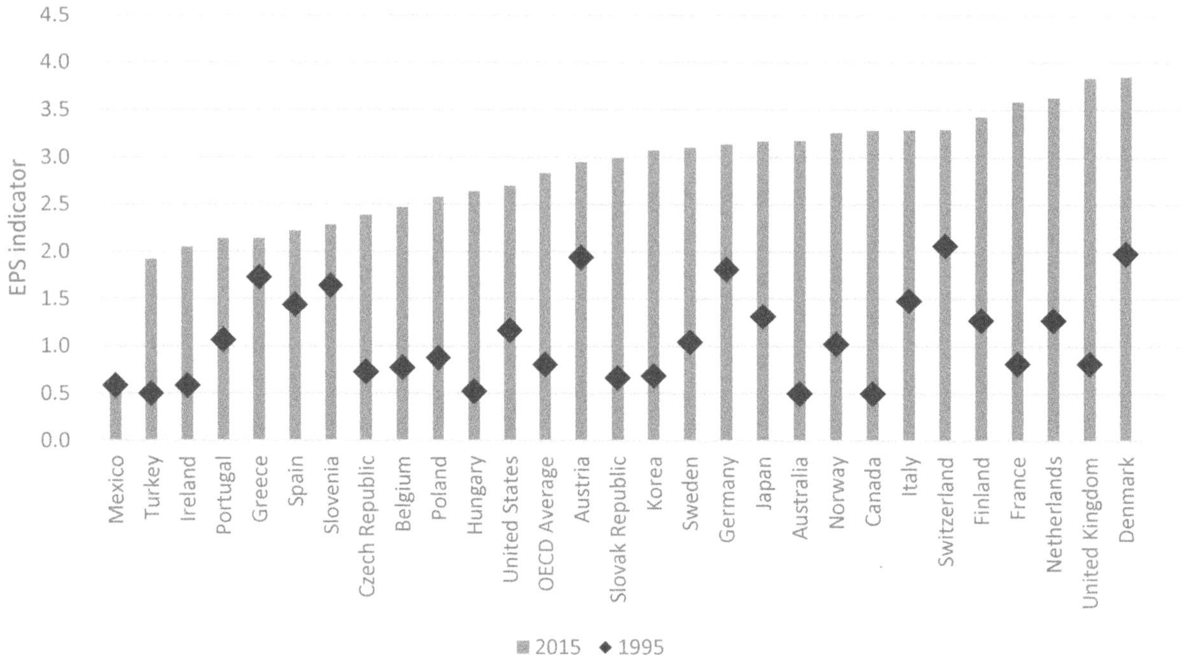

Note: The figure shows the evolution of environmental policy stringency from 1995 (squares) to 2015 (bars). Where no data were available for 2015, the data for 2012 are used. Slovenia's starting value is from the year 2008. See Box 1.3. for more details on the measurement of the environmental policy stringency indicator.
Source: OECD Stats.

These regulatory differences affect relative production costs of firms across countries and sectors, for example, by increasing the price of inputs for firms located in the most stringent jurisdictions. This raises the concern that cross-country differences in environmental policy stringency could impact the competitiveness of affected businesses, particularly in a world characterised by the rise in global value chains and the fragmentation and interdependence of production across multiple jurisdictions.

Due to fears of hurting economic growth and shedding jobs, tightening of environmental policies, in particular policies to mitigate climate change, has been politically difficult. While adapting to new environmental regulations unquestionably requires firms to change parts of their production processes and their business models, it might also lead to efficiency gains through restructuring, and induce new resource- and pollution-saving innovations that could enhance productivity. In spite of these potential positive effects of environmental policies, concerns about their potential negative impacts on firms' economic performance often dominate the public and policy debates. This is reinforced by the slowdown of productivity, the reduction of employment in the manufacturing sector in most advanced economies, the 2008 Global Financial Crisis and the modest rates of economic growth experienced by many OECD countries since then (OECD, 2019[6]; OECD, 2019[7]). Concerns about a loss of competitiveness of local industries have also led to multiple exemptions for particular sectors, jeopardising the environmental ambitions.

Evidence from OECD studies

Empirical evidence about the economic effects of environmental policies is needed to implement better-informed policies. This publication summarises eight recent OECD studies investigating the link between environmental policies and economic outcomes, based on cross-country firm-level, sectoral and macro datasets (see Box 1.2 for a brief description of these studies). A wide range of economic outcomes are considered: productivity, employment, domestic investment, foreign direct investment and international trade. In addition to the economic impacts, three of these studies also examine the effects of environmental policies on polluting emissions, making it possible to analyse these two dimensions jointly. This allows to juxtapose the economic impacts and environmental achievements.

The papers presented in this publication make a common significant contribution to the existing empirical literature: they take a cross-country perspective of the effects of environmental policies, thanks to substantial data collection efforts and the use of comparable policy measures across countries in the analysis. Since firm-level environmental performance data are typically only available from government-owned country-specific datasets, the joint economic and environmental effects are explored instead through country-specific or EU-level case studies.

Is looking at past experience helpful with regard to future environmental policies?

The studies reviewed in this publication leverage on historical changes in the stringency of environmental policies, to analyse their effects on economic outcomes along various dimensions. As shown in Figure 1.2, while the stringency of environmental policy increased substantially over the period 1995-2015, allowing a backward-looking analysis of its effects, the future increases in stringency that are needed to address current challenges, such as climate change, might lie outside past changes. Potential non-linearities in both the economic and environmental effects could thus alter the conclusions drawn from the studies.

What, then, can be learned from past changes with regard to future policies, at a time when many countries around the world are implementing new environmental policies to reduce air pollution, carbon emissions, waste generation and other sources of environmental damage and health risk? In the climate change domain, reaching the ambitious goals of the Paris Agreement is challenging but possible, and does in fact not necessarily imply stronger increases in environmental policy stringency compared to what has been observed over the past decades. As an illustration, Figure 1.3 shows average past annual growth rates of industry energy prices across OECD countries for the period 1995-2014 and compares those with future increases implied by a USD 50/tonne of CO_2 carbon price.[5] It highlights that for the majority of countries, and for OECD countries on average, smaller increases in industry energy prices than those observed in the recent past would be sufficient to reach the targets of the Paris Agreement.[6] These calculations are rather conservative estimates, as they do not incorporate effects of technological break-throughs or consumer responses to higher energy prices. This simple example suggests that looking at past effects of environmental policies, as done by all studies reviewed in this publication, can bring valuable lessons for the future. Nevertheless, such increases are insufficient to achieve full decarbonisation of the economy by 2050.

Figure 1.3. Industry energy prices: Past versus future changes needed to reach a USD 50 per tonne of CO_2 carbon price

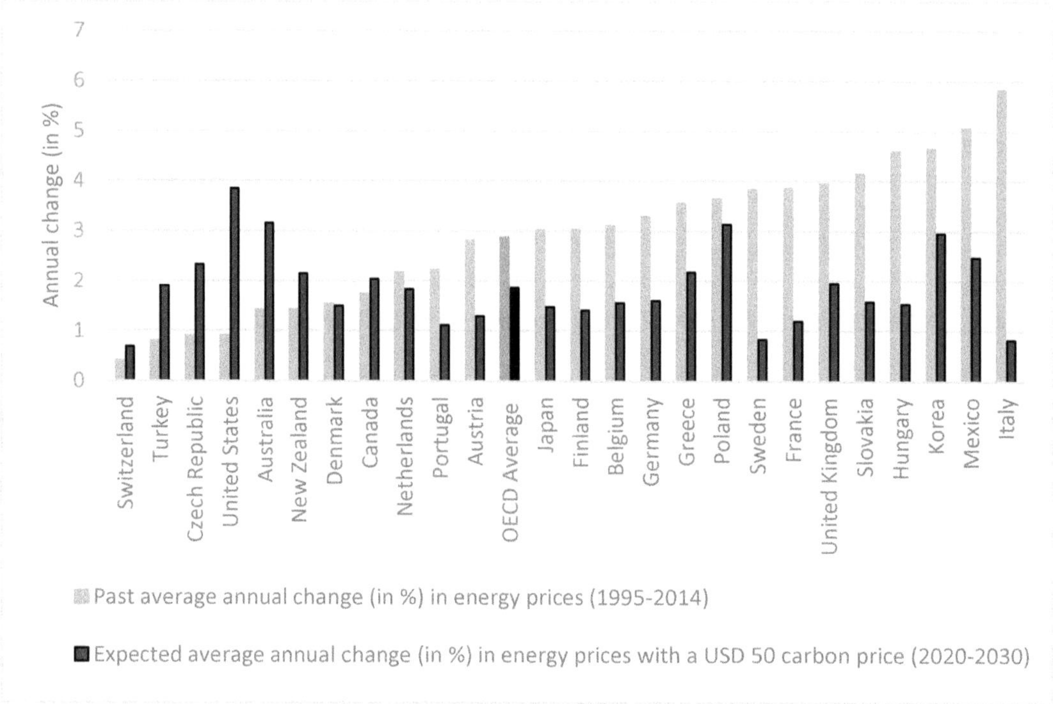

Note: The light blue bars indicate past average annual changes (in %) of industry energy prices over the period 1995-2014. The dark blue bars show expected annual changes of industry energy prices (in %) over the period 2020-30 to reach a USD 50 carbon price. The OECD average is an unweighted average of the 25 countries shown in the graph. Industry energy prices can differ from overall energy prices.[7]
Source: Authors' calculation based on data from Sato et al. (2019[5]).

Box 1.2. OECD studies summarised in this publication

This publication summarises *ex-post* econometric work on the relationship between environmental policies and economic performance for manufacturing industries that has been conducted jointly by the OECD Economics Department and the Environment Directorate over the past years.

- *Productivity:* Albrizio, Koźluk and Zipperer (2017[8]) estimates the effects of environmental policy stringency (as measured by the OECD indicator) on country, industry, and firm-level multifactor productivity (MFP) in 17 OECD countries over the period 1995-2012.
- *Employment:* Dechezleprêtre, Nachtigall and Stadler (2020[9]) examines the effect of changes in energy prices (a proxy for policies aimed at curbing carbon emissions) on employment in the manufacturing sector based on industry-level and firm-level data from 23 OECD countries over the period 2000-14.
- *Investment:* Dlugosch and Koźluk (2017[10]) examines the effect of changes in energy prices on the investment ratio of listed firms over the period 1995-2011 in 30 OECD countries.
- *Foreign direct investment:* Garsous, Koźluk and Dlugosch, (2020[11]) looks at the energy price effect on FDI using data from mandatory balance sheets (share of foreign assets over total assets) of listed companies located in 75 countries over the period 1995-2008.
- *Trade:* Koźluk and Timiliotis (2016[12]) estimates the effect of changes in energy prices on international trade patterns over the period 1990-2009. They use a model of bilateral trade flows between the manufacturing sectors of 23 OECD and 6 BRIICS countries.
- *EU ETS and firm performance:* Dechezleprêtre, Nachtigall and Venmans (2018[13]) examines the effect of the European Union Emissions Trading System on the performance of affected companies in terms of carbon emissions and a range of economic outcomes, such as turnover, employment, investment and profits based on a combination of installation- and firm-level data, using data for 31 European countries over the period 2005-12.
- *Carbon tax and firm performance:* Dussaux (2020[14]) examines the effect of rising energy prices and carbon taxes on the environmental and economic performance of the French manufacturing industry based on firm- and industry-level data over the period 2001-16.
- *Energy prices and firm performance:* Brucal and Dechezleprêtre (2021[15]) analyses the effect of rising energy prices on the environmental and economic performance of the Indonesian manufacturing industry based on firm- and industry-level data over the period of 1980-2015.

The effects of environmental policies on firm behaviour

The effect of environmental policies on environmental and economic outcomes operates through a number of steps, as illustrated in Figure 1.4. When environmental policies are implemented (step 1), polluting facilities have to undertake pollution abatement activities, often imposing additional costs on businesses.[8] Depending on the design of the policy, firms can react with different types of responses. The policy might, for instance, simply require installing a filter on a chimney (so called end-of-pipe abatement). It may, however, also require more substantive adjustments, such as changes in the whole production process, or innovations in the product mix (step 2). The restructuring measures can also imply a reallocation of resources (step 3). This can imply additional investment, changes to the configuration of supply chains, adjusting the number of employees, or a combination of these responses. Once resources are reallocated, in the last step of Figure 1.4, the results of the changed processes will be seen in the environmental and economic performance of firms or industries, e.g. emission levels, productivity or profits.

Figure 1.4. How effects of environmental policies develop

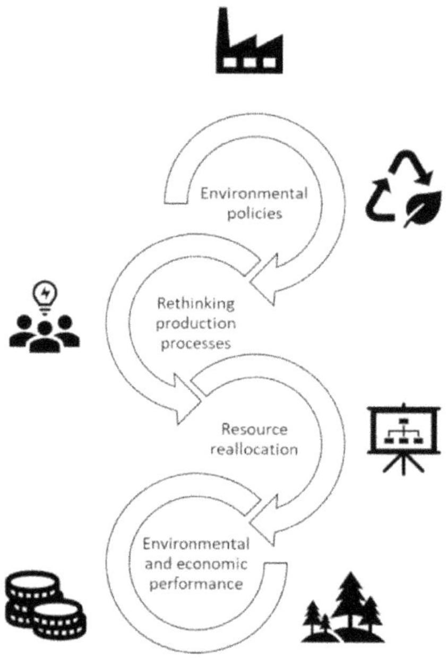

The Pollution Haven and Porter hypotheses: the corner stones of predictions of the economic effects of environmental policies

The theoretical literature on the relationship between environmental policies and economic outcomes provides various predictions about the direction of the economic effects on firms, which are based on two main hypotheses. The so-called "Pollution Haven Hypothesis" (McGuire, 1982[16]) suggests that differences in the stringency of environmental policies across countries will shift pollution-intensive production capacity towards regions with less stringent regulation, where firms enjoy a newly acquired competitive advantage. Thus domestic reductions in pollution levels will be accompanied by increasing emissions in other regions, which is particularly troubling in the case of global pollutants such as carbon dioxide. On the other hand, the so-called "Porter Hypothesis" (Porter, 1991[17]; Porter and van der Linde, 1995[18]) suggests that stringent environmental policies could stimulate productivity growth via efficiency improvements and innovations aimed at avoiding these cost burdens and meeting the cleaner standards set by public policies. Porter argues that firms do not always make optimal decisions and that incomplete information, weak competition, organisational inertia and other behavioural biases may prevent firms from exploiting all profitable innovation opportunities. Environmental policies may thereby help firms to overcome such challenges. Induced innovations in environmentally-friendly technologies could thus lead to a better economic performance, offsetting the additional costs.

Different predictions for different aggregation levels

The validity of these theoretical predictions about the economic effects of environmental policies can differ depending on the level of aggregation, and a negative impact on facilities targeted by environmental policies need not translate into the same negative effect at the macro level. For example, an inefficient plant might need to close down, but the performance of the operating firm owning the plant overall might improve as a consequence. Resources of the inefficient plant may, for example, be used more productively in other plants of the firms. Similarly, sectoral outcomes can hide market dynamics and factor reallocation between individual firms. At the macroeconomic level, taking into account general equilibrium effects, a sectoral decline can be outweighed by another sector's improvement. Closure of inefficient plants might change the competition structure, which could lead to increased production and overall pollution (Qiu, Zhou and Wei, 2018[19]; Guarini, 2020[20]). It is therefore important to analyse the economic effects at different aggregation levels in order to obtain a complete picture of the effects.

Predictions for individual economic outcomes

Taking a closer look at the various economic outcomes discussed in the following chapters, theory typically does not provide a clear-cut prediction of the effect. This underlines the importance of providing empirical evidence.

Productivity, the first outcome studied in this publication, could be expected to increase according to the Porter Hypothesis. However, the additional investment in pollution-control technologies might crowd out more productive investment, potentially causing a productivity slowdown for these firms (Morgenstern, Pizer and Shih, 2002[21]).[9] This holds in particular within the conventional view that firms are perfectly rational and exhaust all profitable investment opportunities. Policy-induced investment in pollution-control technologies could then divert capital from more profitable investments. At the industry level, productivity might, however, still rise if the least productive firms are driven out of the market.

The second outcome studied in this volume is employment. While there might be adjustment costs in the short term, in the long run, there should be no sustained effects on employment as labour should simply shift from polluting to less polluting sectors (Chateau, Bibas and Lanzi, 2018[22]; Fankhauser, Sehhleier and Stern, 2008[23]). The short-term effects could be positive if non-polluting production is more labour-intensive than polluting activities, or negative in case a contraction of output leads to employment losses. For policy making, particular challenges occur, if such job losses are geographically clustered in areas dependent on pollution-intensive industries (Morgenstern, Pizer and Shih, 2002[21]; Kahn and Mansur, 2013[24]).

Whether investment decreases or increases in response to environmental regulation depends on the downsizing and modernisation effects (Xepapadeas and de Zeeuw, 1998[25]). On the one hand, input costs might rise, leading to increased production costs and decreased output via a downsizing effect, eventually lowering investment. On the other hand, increased input costs might encourage firms to switch from old, often energy-intensive machines to new, more energy-efficient ones. Such a modernisation effect could increase overall investment.

Foreign direct investment is the fourth outcome examined here, and theoretical predictions are more univocal in this case. Following the Pollution Haven Hypothesis described above, theory predicts that tighter environmental policies should provide incentives for firms to relocate parts of their production to countries with laxer regulations (McGuire, 1982[16]; Xing and Kolstad, 2002[26]). This is especially relevant for pollution-intensive industries and can potentially lead to carbon leakage, whereby part of the emissions avoided through domestic environmental regulations are simply shifted to other locations.

Trade through global value chains (GVCs) is the fifth outcome studied in this publication. Similar to the predictions about foreign direct investment, off-shoring incentives for firms might lead to more trade through GVCs, e.g. importing pollution-intensive inputs from other countries. However, increased efficiency and productivity through a Porter effect might increase the competitiveness of firms, potentially providing them with a comparative advantage in cleaner production processes and increasing exports in "cleaner" goods.

Measuring environmental policy stringency

A challenge common to any analysis investigating the effects of environmental policies is to measure and quantify these policies accurately. Comparable cross-country measures are often not readily available, leading many studies to draw on country- or sector-specific policies, providing results that are not easily generalisable. Two measures are used in most of the studies presented in this publication, which are both relatively well comparable across countries and time, namely energy prices and an aggregate indicator for the stringency of environmental policies developed by the OECD.

Since climate change policies such as carbon taxes or cap-and-trade mechanisms primarily affect firms through raising energy prices (Aldy and Pizer, 2015[27]), industrial energy prices have emerged as an oft-used proxy for climate policy stringency. While there are common factors that affect energy prices globally, such as crude oil and gas prices, there is considerable variation in energy prices across countries and sectors because of energy taxes or limited integration of energy markets due to transport costs or infrastructure bottlenecks. This variation can be exploited to determine the effect of energy prices on economic outcomes. A major advantage of using energy prices is that they are directly comparable across countries and time. They are also available for a large set of countries and are directly observed at the country-sector level.

However, energy prices offer only a partial measure of environmental policy stringency. In particular, they do not capture non-market-based environmental policies such as command-and-control instruments (e.g. emission standards, air pollutant maximum concentration levels) which do not impact the energy input prices directly. For this reason, the OECD has developed a composite indicator of environmental policy stringency (the EPS index) to provide a reasonably comparable cross-country measure of both market-based and non-market based policy instruments. The EPS index covers a broad set of climate and energy policies, including market-based instruments which assign an explicit price to environmental externalities, and non-market instruments such as standards (Box 1.3). The studies presented in this publication use either industry energy prices or the EPS index, depending on data availability at the time of the studies. Furthermore, the EPS index is available at the country-year level, whereas energy price data varies at country-sector-year level, allowing for more granular analysis.[10]

Box 1.3. The OECD Environmental Policy Stringency indicator

In order to assess the impact of environmental policy on economic outcomes, a first step is to quantify its stringency. The OECD Environmental Policy Stringency (EPS) index (Botta and Koźluk, 2014[28]) is a unique indicator, which allows for reasonably good comparisons both across countries and across time. The Environmental Policy Stringency index is based on the taxonomy developed by (De Serres, Murtin and Nicoletti, 2010[29]) and aggregated along a tree structure where the sub-components are all weighted equally. A market-based sub-component group of instruments, which assign an explicit price to environmental externalities (taxes on CO_2, SO_X, NO_X and diesel fuel; trading schemes for CO_2, renewable energy certificates, and energy efficiency certificates; feed-in-tariffs; and deposit-refund-schemes), while the non-market component clusters command-and-control instruments, such as standards (emission limit values for NO_X, SO_X and PM, limits on sulphur content in diesel), and technology-support policies, such as government R&D subsidies. The score assigns values from 0 (lowest) to 6 (highest) (see Figure 1.5 for the weighting scheme). A higher value indicates stronger or more stringent policies.

Figure 1.5. Structure of the Environmental Policy Stringency indicator (EPS)

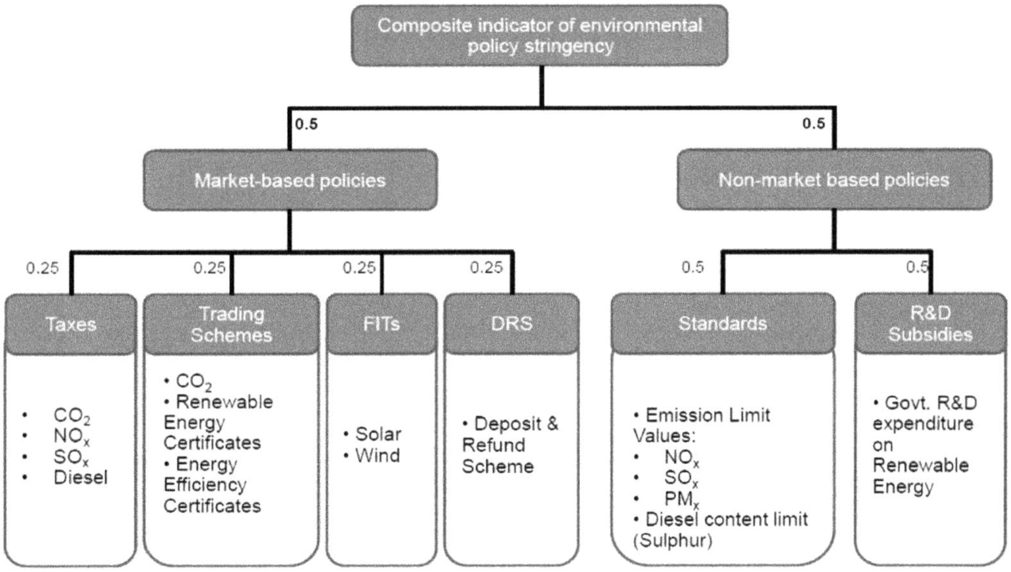

Source: Botta and Koźluk (2014).

The EPS mainly measures the stringency of climate change and air pollution policies at the country-level, mainly upstream. While this has advantages (for example, the effects of upstream regulations flow downstream as well), the main limitation is that the indicator varies only at the country level. Albrizio, Koźluk and Zipperer (2017[8]) introduce the approach that firms are exposed to environmental policies to a different extent, which they term "environmental dependence". This is either defined as pollution intensity (emissions over value added) or energy intensity (energy consumption over value added) of a sector. Interacting the environmental dependence with the EPS indicator yields a sector-specific measure of environmental policy stringency.

Economic impacts from environmental policies – empirical evidence from OECD studies

Technologically-advanced industries and firms benefit in the short-run from environmental policies in terms of productivity gains

Potential productivity gains as a result of tighter environmental policies have triggered much literature since the formulation of the Porter Hypothesis. However, empirical evidence has been rather country- or regulation-specific so far. Albrizio, Koźluk and Zipperer (2017[8]), summarised in Chapter 2, use a panel of OECD countries in their analysis and find that industry and firm productivity responses to environmental policies are heterogeneous, depending on the stage of technological advancement of sectors and firms. The study finds that, at the industry level, productivity growth increases in response to more stringent environmental policy, especially in countries where the industry is close to the global technological frontier (Figure 1.6, left hand side panel). The positive effect on industry productivity diminishes as the distance to the global technology frontier increases and vanishes far from the frontier. Thus, in each industry, the most productive countries benefit most in terms of productivity growth, perhaps because, in these countries, firms have access to the best technologies and are most capable to adapt to new regulations, for example, by improving production processes. They may also have the best access to financial markets, and hence be better able to react to the policy change.[11] Moreover, the productivity effect following an environmental policy change also differs depending on exposure to the policy, as measured by energy-and emissions-intensity. Energy-intensive industries (which are more exposed to environmental policies) and non-energy-intensive industries (which are less exposed) both experience productivity gains, but the effect is around twice as large for energy-intensive industries.

Figure 1.6. More stringent environmental policy is related to higher industry and firm productivity, but only close to the productivity frontier

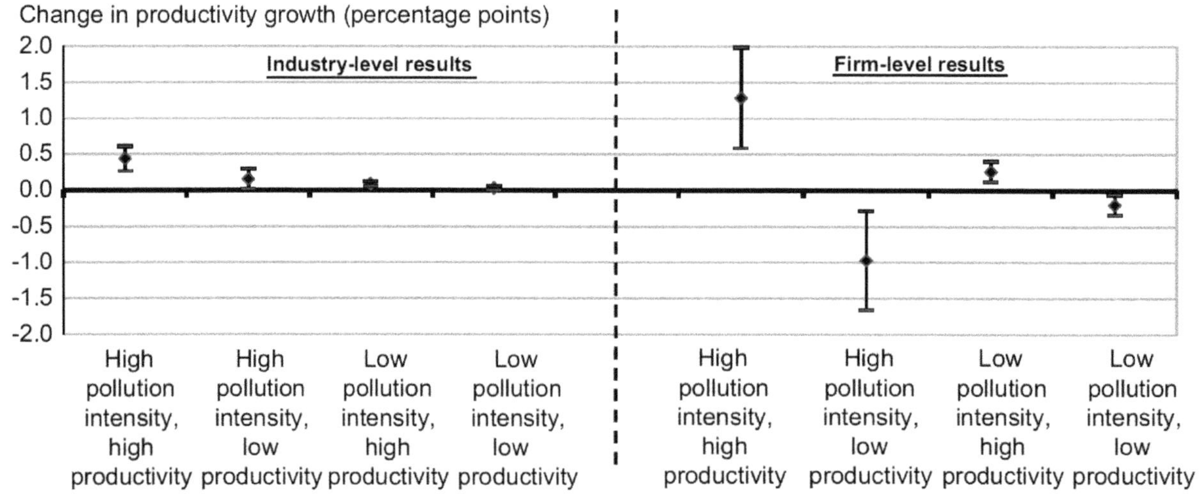

Note: (1) One-year effect of a mean in-sample increase in environmental policy stringency, i.e. 0.12 change in the value of the EPS index in one single year. Effects on productivity growth are estimated to last for three years after the policy change and then fade away: (2) High (low) pollution intensity is defined as an industry with the highest (lowest) pollution intensity on seven selected key pollutants with respect to value added. (3) High productivity is defined as the country-industry pair (or firm) on or close to the estimated global industry (or firm) productivity frontier. Low productivity is defined as country-industry pair (or firm) at the 70th percentile of distance to the global industry (or firm) productivity frontier. (4) 90% confidence intervals are reported.
Source: Albrizio, Koźluk and Zipperer (2017[8]).

At the firm-level, the study finds only partially consistent results with the industry-level: A tightening of environmental policies leads to an increase in the productivity growth of firms close to the technology frontier, but to a decrease in productivity growth for those further away from the frontier (Figure 1.6, right panel). Only one-fifth of the firms are estimated to benefit from environmental policies, while the bottom 30% of firms are hurt in terms of productivity growth. Since smaller firms tend to be further away from the productivity frontier, they are more exposed to the negative effects, possibly because they have limited resources to adapt to the policy changes.

Comparing firm and industry-level results on the productivity effects of environmental policies suggests that part of the adjustment, particularly for less technologically advanced firms, may take the form of firm exit. The exit of the least efficient firms would raise overall industry productivity, cancelling out the negative productivity effects observed in surviving, less efficient firms. Indeed, one may consider the negative effect on the least productive firms as one way to reallocate resources previously locked in firms that were at the margin of exit (Andrews, McGowan and Millot, 2017[30]).

Similar to Albrizio, Koźluk and Zipperer (2017[8]), the broader literature finds heterogeneous effects of environmental policies on productivity. In the short run, environmental policies can have negative effects on productivity in some sectors, and positive impacts in others. The sign of the effects can also vary across pollutants, countries and time. The existing evidence is largely limited to the short run – typically for up to five years. Further work is needed in particular to better understand the long-run effects of environmental policies on productivity, and to understand the underlying reasons for the heterogeneity of results across sectors, pollutants, countries and time (Dechezleprêtre et al., 2019[31]).

Environmental policies have heterogeneous effects on employment, inducing job reallocation between energy-intensive and non-energy-intensive sectors

The effect of environmental policies on employment is a source of major concern, as even small but localised effects can generate strong resistance to policy implementation. The work by Dechezleprêtre, Nachtigall and Stadler (2020[9]), summarised in Chapter 3, shows that, at the sector level, increases in energy prices and in the stringency of environmental policies have a negative and statistically significant impact on total employment in the manufacturing sector. The overall magnitude is small, however: a 10% increase in energy prices leads to a reduction of manufacturing employment by 0.7%. To put things in perspective, job losses linked with increases in energy prices observed over the last two decades in OECD countries are estimated to be respectively 30% and 80% smaller than those due to automation and globalisation. Moreover, these job losses might be partially or completely offset by hires in non-manufacturing sectors, which are not considered in the study. Energy-intensive sectors (e.g. non-metallic minerals, iron and steel) are most affected, while the impact is not statistically significant for less energy-intensive sectors (Figure 1.7.). Even in energy-intensive sectors, however, the size of the effect is relatively small: in iron and steel production – the most affected sector – a 10% increase in the price of energy reduces manufacturing employment by 1.9% in the short run.

Figure 1.7. Short-term employment effect of a 10% increase in energy prices across sectors

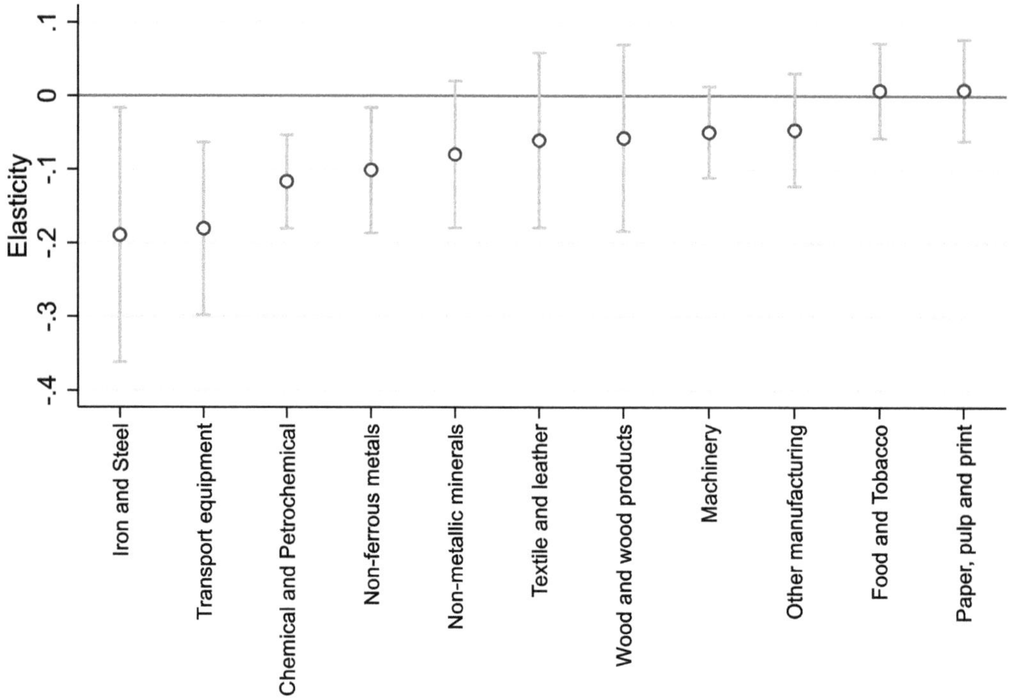

Note: The figure shows the effect of a 10% increase in energy prices and 95% confidence intervals of the energy price variable on the log of employment. These underlying models are estimated with a one-year time lag. For the iron and steel sector, a 10% increase in energy prices leads to nearly 2% decline in employment.
Source: Dechezleprêtre, Nachtigall and Stadler (2020[9]).

At the micro level, the results show that higher energy prices have a statistically significant and small *positive* effect on the employment of surviving firms. However, these average effects at the firm level again hide important heterogeneity. In particular sub-sectors (e.g. basic chemicals), even surviving firms suffer and lay off workers because of higher energy prices and stricter environmental policies. The contrasting results of higher energy prices at the sector- and firm-level can be reconciled by looking at business dynamics. An analysis on the energy price effect on firm exit and entry shows that higher energy prices increase the probability of firm exit. Accelerated firm exit allows surviving firms to expand, boosting firm-level employment. Contrary to higher energy prices, stricter environmental policies (including both taxation and non-market regulations) reduce employment of surviving firms. Looking at business dynamics, stricter environmental policies do not affect entry or exit of firms, explaining why the negative effect on employment at the sector-level mirrors the negative effect at the firm-level.

Two country-specific studies summarised in this publication also find evidence of small aggregate effects on employment, with important heterogeneity in job reallocation across firms. Dussaux (2020[14]), summarised in Chapter 8, investigates the impact of energy prices on employment in the French manufacturing sector and finds that rising energy prices do not affect total manufacturing employment. However, employment in large and energy-inefficient surviving firms declines while employment increases in energy-efficient firms, notably SMEs. Similarly, Brucal and Dechezleprêtre (2021[15]), summarised in Chapter 9, looking at the Indonesian manufacturing sector, find small increases in employment among small plants and slight reductions in employment in larger firms, but no effect overall at the manufacturing level. Other empirical papers (Aldy and Pizer, 2015[27]; Dechenes, 2011[32]; Yamazaki, 2017[33]) and OECD modelling studies (Chateau, Bibas and Lanzi, 2018[22]) have similarly found small negative or statistically insignificant effects of environmental policies or energy prices on employment. Such aggregate effects mask significant heterogeneity across firms and sectors, underlining the importance of combining both sector- and firm-level analysis.

In summary, the OECD studies find that past environmental policies have not had large impacts on overall employment in manufacturing industries, despite heterogeneities across sectors. The most energy-intensive as well as the least productive firms tend to experience declines in employment. At the same time, less energy-intensive or more productive firms may benefit and increase employment. Relocation barriers tend to be higher across countries, for example, due to cross-country differences in industry laws. Hence, relocation effects tend to be larger within countries, rather than across countries (Dechezleprêtre et al., 2019[31]; Dechezleprêtre and Sato, 2017[34]). Importantly, the job reallocation rates potentially triggered by environmental policies that raise energy prices are relatively small compared to historical reallocation rates. OECD global simulations (Chateau, Bibas and Lanzi, 2018[22]) show that over the long run, a USD 50/tCO_2 carbon tax implemented in all regions of the world would trigger a reallocation of only around 0.3% of jobs for OECD countries (and 0.8% of jobs for non-OECD countries, because the heavily impacted sectors (energy-intensive sectors) represent only a small share of total employment (82% of the largest CO_2 emitting non-agricultural sectors account for only 8% of total jobs in the average OECD country). In comparison, job reallocation rates averaged 20% of the labour force over the period 1995-2005 in OECD Member countries.

The job reallocation rates triggered by environmental policies also appear small when compared with the potential effects of other major macroeconomic trends. One example of such a trend is the diffusion of new information and communication technologies, which are likely to radically change the type of jobs that will be needed in the future, and how, where and by whom they will be undertaken. For instance, an OECD study based on the OECD's Survey of Adult Skills (PIAAC), estimates that 9% of existing jobs are at a high risk of being automated (Arntz, Gregory and Zierahn, 2016[35]) and 25% of jobs will be changed fundamentally.

Domestic investment suffers, firms invest more abroad

By requiring polluting companies to make their production process less emission-intensive, environmental policies likely affect investment decisions. The overall effect could be neutral – simply reorienting investment toward less polluting production technologies – but investment in firms affected by environmental regulations could also be discouraged. Dlugosch and Koźluk (2017[10]), summarised in Chapter 4, point to a decline in domestic investment across all manufacturing sectors and to an increase in FDI by firms operating in energy-intensive sectors, possibly reflecting the search for "pollution havens". The analysis is based on balance sheets of listed companies in the manufacturing sector located in 75 countries and focuses on changes in the total investment ratio (i.e. the share of domestic and foreign investment in total assets) following an increase in relative energy prices.

On average, energy prices are associated with lower total investment, but there is significant heterogeneity across sectors. Dlugosch and Koźluk (2017[10]) find that a 10% increase in relative energy prices leads to a 1% decrease in investment on average in the manufacturing sector. However, this result masks significant heterogeneity across sectors: increasing energy prices, which decrease investment in low and medium energy-intensity industries, but increase it in high energy-intensity industries (Figure 1.8.). Their results suggest that in the sectors with a high energy-intensity the effect to modernise machines and equipment is strong and increases overall investment. In sectors with a low energy-intensity, investments are reduced as a response to the increase in energy input costs. Energy is a less important input for these firms, and incentives to modernise energy-consuming equipment are lower. In firms with a low energy intensity, it may also be more difficult to reduce the energy consumption further because energy may be consumed with low intensity across many different parts of the production process. The energy-consuming production may not be at the heart of the business model, making it more difficult to mobilise financial resources to invest in more energy efficient technologies. However, the fall in investment in low energy-intensity sectors, which suffer most, is still quite modest: for a large increase in energy prices (from median to the 75th percentile) of the price distribution across sectors and countries, their investment decreases by 0.12 percentage points (relative to an average investment ratio of 5.6%).

Dechezleprêtre, Nachtigall and Venmans (2018[13]), summarised in Chapter 7, also find that energy-intensive firms regulated by the EU ETS increase their investments (likely in low-carbon technologies), and Brucal and Dechezleprêtre (2021[15]), summarised in Chapter 9, provide evidence that Indonesian firms invest in more energy-efficient machinery and vehicles in response to higher energy prices.

Figure 1.8. Increases in energy prices barely affect total investment but decrease domestic investment in all sectors

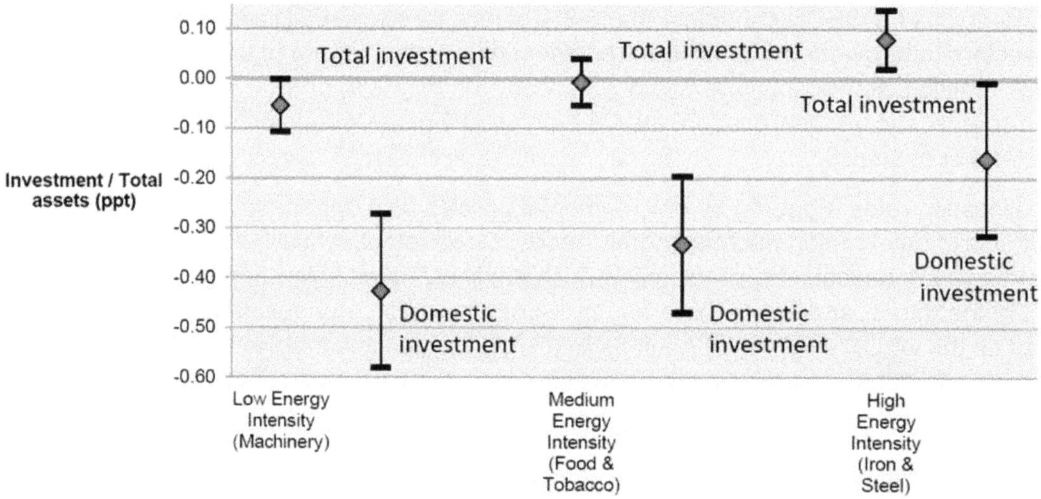

Note: The dots represent the estimated effects of a change of energy price growth from the median (Poland) to the 75th percentile (Germany) for different values of energy intensity. Values on the vertical axis are expressed in percentage points. For example, at low levels of energy intensity a change of energy price growth from the median to the 75th percentile is associated with a 0.42 percentage point decline in the investment ratio (investment / total assets). The black lines indicate the 90% confidence intervals.
Source: Dlugosch and Koźluk (2017[10]).

Overall, the size of these estimated effects is quite small, especially when compared with the effects of other structural policies that either deter or encourage investment. The econometric results show that changes in energy prices explain a very small part of changes in domestic investment. Other factors, included as control variables – such as macroeconomic trends or changes in employment protection legislation – had a much larger effect on investment between 1990 and 2012 than energy prices.

The positive effect on total investment for energy-intensive industries found by Dlugosch and Koźluk (2017[10]) in their global study appears to be driven by an increase in the amount of foreign investment, perhaps in countries where environmental policies are laxer (and energy prices lower). Indeed, Dlugosch and Koźluk (2017[10]) split investment into its domestic and its foreign components and find that environmental policy decreases domestic investment, regardless of energy intensity (Figure 1.8.). This discrepancy between the effect on total and on domestic investment points to an effect on foreign investment. This hypothesis is directly tested by Garsous, Koźluk and Dlugosch (2020[11]), summarised in Chapter 5, using changes in relative energy prices as the main explanatory variable. They show that a 10% increase in relative energy prices leads to an increase of 0.5 percentage points in the ratio between foreign and total assets, from a mean of 14% in the first year after the price increase. The effect increases over a longer time horizon to about 0.75 percentage points. This effect on FDI is more pronounced in energy-intensive sectors: a 10% increase in energy prices, which are affected by energy taxes, carbon pricing and other environmental policy instruments to reduce pollution associated with fossil fuel energy consumption, increases outward FDI by about 1.1 percentage points for these sectors. Based on their empirical model, Garsous, Koźluk and Dlugosch (2020[11]) simulate the effect on FDI of introducing a modest (USD 15/tCO_2) and a large (USD 55/tCO_2) carbon tax in the industry. Even a large carbon tax was found to have a small effect on FDI.

The broader literature on the effects of environmental regulation on FDI remains inconclusive. Most studies find that environmental policies either have no significant effect on FDI or lead at most to small increases in foreign assets, in line with Dlugosch and Koźluk (2017[10]) and Garsous, Koźluk and Dlugosch (2020[11]). In a review of the literature, Dechezleprêtre and Sato (2017[34]) show that the overall conclusions are sensitive to the geographic coverage, the type of environmental regulation, and the empirical specification, including the data and use of control variables. Thus, it seems that concerns regarding the adverse effects of environmental policies via this "pollution haven" channel are likely to be somewhat overstated.

Overall trade flows are barely affected, with rising exports of low-pollution sectors and declining exchanges of high-pollution ones

Another major source of policy concern is that stringent environmental policies may affect the competitiveness of regulated firms and thus their export market share. Yet, using trade data from 23 OECD countries and 10 manufacturing industries, Koźluk and Timiliotis (2016[12]), summarised in Chapter 6, find that, overall, environmental policies (as measured by the OECD EPS indicator described in Box 1.3) have had little effect on trade measured either in terms of gross exports or in terms of the domestic value added embedded in exports (which accounts for the rise in global value chains that increasingly decouple gross exports from trade in value added).[12] In line with priors, they also find that environmental policies affect more strongly the domestic value added export component than gross exports. This is expected because gross exports include to a large share imported intermediate components, which are not exposed to the domestic environmental policy.

As with other effects of environmental policies, this overall finding masks heterogeneous impacts on sectors depending on their pollution intensity. When environmental policies become more stringent in the exporting country, exports of high-pollution sectors decline, whereas exports of lower-pollution sectors increase, in line with basic trade theory. The latter finding echoes some earlier work suggesting that more stringent environmental policies may be associated with higher exports of so-called environmental goods (Sauvage, 2014[36]). Measured in terms of value added, the negative effect on pollution-intensive industries is counterbalanced by a positive effect on low-pollution industries of the same magnitude, both strongly significant (Figure 1.9).

Figure 1.9. Environmental policy decreases exports in high pollution industries and increases exports in low pollution industries

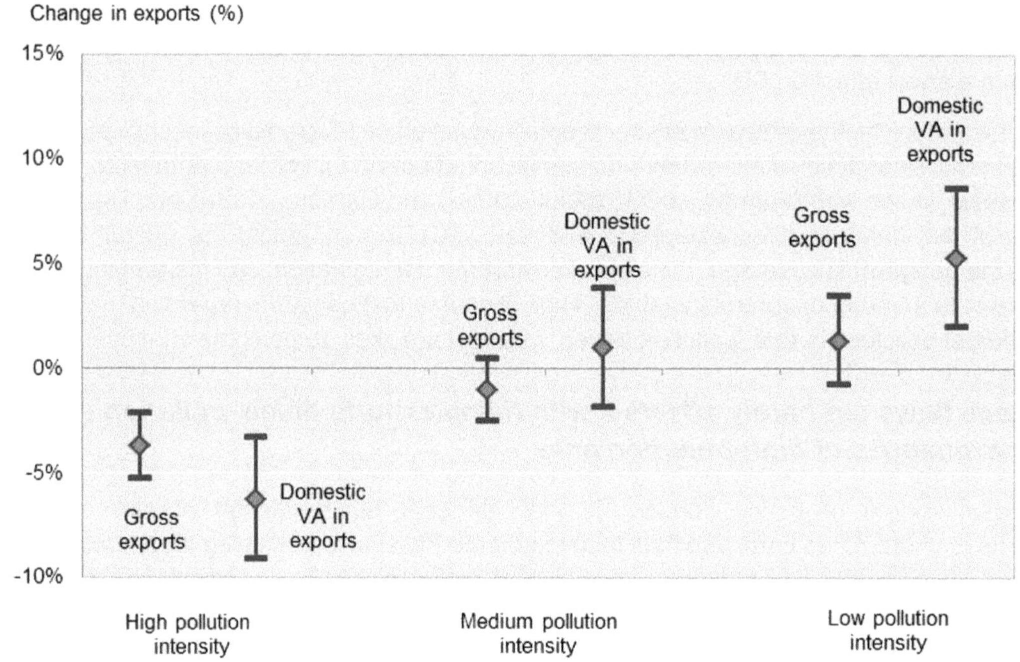

Note: The figure shows the effect on trade flows (exports from one country to another) associated with a change in the comparative environmental policy stringency between two countries. The dots represent the estimated effects of a change in the comparative environmental policy stringency on the trade performance. The change in environmental policy stringency compares two countries in which policies are equally stringent (median) to a situation in which the difference is large (75th percentile of distribution of difference). Effects are shown for three types of sectors with a high, medium or low pollution intensity. The blue lines indicate the 90% confidence intervals. The estimated coefficients are short-term effects (1 year lag).
Source: Koźluk and Timiliotis (2016[12]).

These findings suggest that, ceteris paribus, increased regulatory stringency in one country (for example, Denmark, Germany or Switzerland which tend to have a higher environmental policy stringency) leads foreign countries (e.g. the BRIICS countries - Brazil, Russia, India, Indonesia and China - which tend to have a lower environmental policy stringency) to specialise in the production of polluting goods which they can subsequently export back to "virtuous" countries (Levinson and Taylor, 2008[37]). This concern is particularly troubling for environmental policy aimed at addressing global environmental problems such as climate change, since pollution may simply be shifted to another region, with the same effects on global environmental degradation. However, the change in comparative advantage of polluting industries is estimated to be relatively small compared to other factors affecting trade. Focusing on trade between OECD and emerging countries over the 1995-2008 period, Figure 1.10 shows the size of the effect on exports from high-pollution industries in OECD countries toward emerging economies and compares this with the impact on low-pollution industries, accounting for differences in the stringency of environmental policies in these two groups of countries. The three colours show the effect of environmental policy (red: negative and green: positive), the effect of changing tariff structures (dark blue) and other effects, such as capital and labour endowment or institutional quality (light blue). The adverse effects of environmental policy on high-pollution sectors are not only compensated by positive effects on low-pollution industries, but also dwarfed by the effects of past tariff liberalisations and other factors.

These results confirm previous research focusing on how imports and bilateral trade flows are affected by environmental policy, which finds no aggregate effect at the country level and only a limited effect on energy-intensive industries (Aldy and Pizer, 2015[27]; Branger, Quirion and Chevallier, 2017[38]). In related work, Sato and Dechezleprêtre (2015[39]) conclude that energy price differences between countries only explain 0.01 percent of the variation in trade flows. Thus, trade is barely affected by environmental policies. Dechezleprêtre and Sato (2017[34]) draw similar conclusions after a review of the "pollution haven" literature that analyses trade patterns. In response to stricter environmental regulation, imports of pollution-intensive goods tend to increase. The effect is, however, small and concentrated in a few sectors. Other determinants of trade flows tend to dominate the effect of environmental policy stringency. Levinson (2010[40]) for instance argues that any "pollution haven" effect is likely overwhelmed by factors such as the cost and availability of skilled workers, raw materials, transport costs and the overall market structure.

Figure 1.10. Environmental policy has small effects on trade patterns, even in pollution-intensive sectors

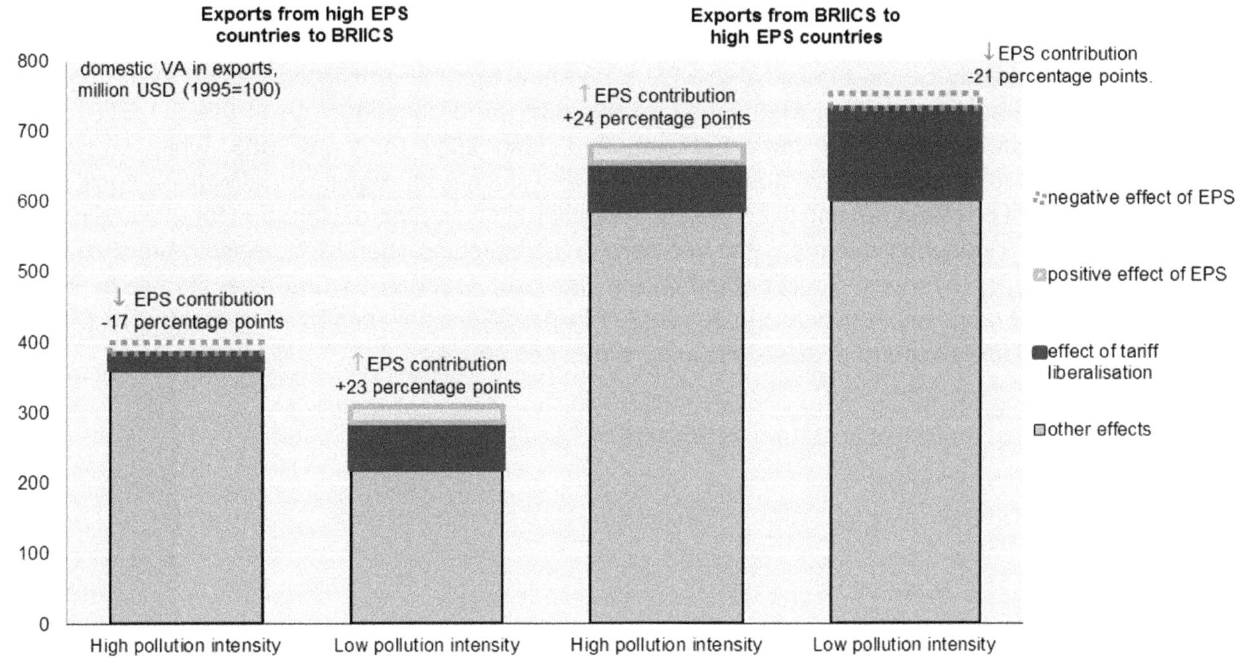

Note: The figure shows the export increase from 1995 to 2008, between high EPS countries and BRIICS countries (typically with low EPS scores) in high- and low- pollution-intensity sectors. The green rectangles indicate increase in exports caused by differences in environmental policy stringency. The red indicates lost export due to differences in environmental policies. The dark blue parts show the effect of tariff liberalisations and the light blue shows other effects.

Source: Koźluk and Timiliotis (2016[12]).

Are the economic effects small only because the effects on environmental outcomes are small? Joint analysis of economic and environmental impacts

The results of the studies summarised in this publication show that environmental policies do not hurt economic performance significantly, but induce factor reallocations both within and across sectors, generating winners and losers. But are these small average effects – even if they hide important heterogeneity – a simple consequence of lax environmental policies? If this is the case, then more stringent policies in the future might have larger adverse consequences on the economy. To answer this question, empirical analyses of the effects of environmental policies need to look *jointly* at economic and environmental performance. Three studies summarised in this publication carry out such an empirical analysis of the joint environmental and economic effects of climate change policies and energy prices, providing insights into the full impact of environmental policies on environmental targets (their primary objective) and economic performance.

The European Union Emissions Trading System and its economic and environmental impacts

Dechezleprêtre, Nachtigall and Venmans (2018[13]), summarised in Chapter 7, provide a comprehensive firm-level impact evaluation of the effects of the EU's Emission Trading System (ETS) on carbon emissions and economic outcomes. The EU ETS is the European Union's flagship climate policy instrument and is the largest carbon market in the world, covering more than 12 000 plants in 31 countries (Laing et al., 2014[41]). Dechezleprêtre, Nachtigall and Venmans (2018[13]) recover the causal effect of the EU ETS on regulated companies by comparing them with unregulated, but similar firms and installations in terms of economic variables and emissions before the policy implementation (a "matching" method), examining effects on firms' emissions, revenues, employment, investment and profits.

The results of the study on the effects of the EU ETS show that the emissions trading system led to a substantial reduction of emissions. Figure 1.11 shows that, as a consequence of the EU ETS, carbon emissions were on average 10% lower between 2005 and 2012 than pre-2005, while employment remained unaffected. In addition, the study did not find any statistically significant effects on firms' profits, but a positive effect on revenues and fixed assets of regulated firms. One explanation for this finding could be that the EU ETS induced investment into low-carbon technologies, thereby increasing productivity and thus leading to higher revenues. Similar effects have also been found in country-level studies by Wagner et al. (2014[42]) for France, by Petrick and Wagner (2014[43]) for Germany, and by Klemetsen et al. (2020[44]) for Norway (see Dechezleprêtre et al. (2019[31]) for a detailed review).

Figure 1.11. Environmental and economic effects of the EU ETS

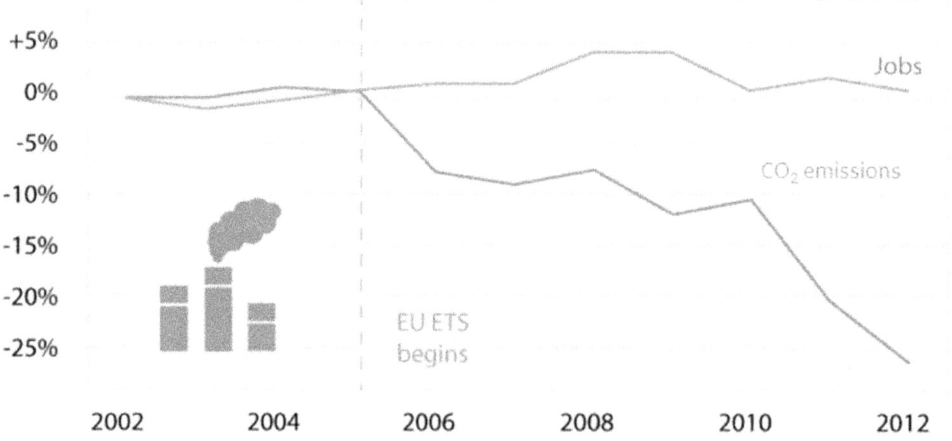

Note: The figure shows the causal year-specific impact of participation in the EU ETS on CO_2 emissions of regulated plants and number of employees of their mother companies by year. Over the period 2005-12, the average treatment effect is +2% for employment (not statistically significant) and -10% for CO_2 emissions.
Source: Based on Dechezleprêtre, Nachtigall and Venmans (2018[13]).

The joint effects of energy prices and carbon taxes in the French manufacturing sector

Dussaux (2020[14]), summarised in Chapter 8, investigates the effects of energy prices on energy use, carbon emissions, employment, output and investment in the French manufacturing sector. The study shows that, at the firm level, a 10% increase in energy costs results in a 6% decline in energy use, a 9% decrease in carbon emissions, and a 2% decrease in the number of full-time employees within one year.

However, these jobs are not lost, but are reallocated to other firms. At the industry level, the study finds no statistical link between energy prices and net job impacts, indicating that jobs lost at affected firms are compensated by increases in employment in other firms operating in the same sector during the same year. On average, large and energy-intensive firms experience a greater reduction in carbon emissions and greater job reallocation than smaller and energy-efficient firms.

The paper is able to measure the causal effect of the French carbon tax on the aggregate manufacturing sector since its introduction in 2014. Figure 1.12 plots the carbon tax on the left axis (green line) together with the impact of the carbon tax on the French manufacturing sector's jobs (purple line) and carbon emissions (red line) on the right axis. In five years, the carbon tax decreased carbon emissions by 5%. The net effect on employment is much smaller in magnitude and even slightly positive at 0.8%.

Figure 1.12. The impact of the French carbon tax on aggregate jobs and CO_2 emissions

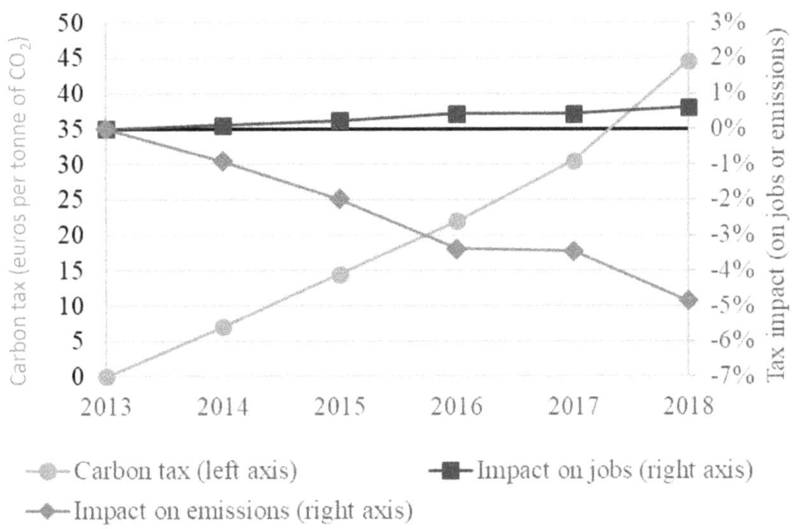

Note: The figure shows the simulated impact of the carbon tax on the number of jobs and CO_2 emissions of the French manufacturing sector.
Source: Dussaux (2020[14]).

The joint effects of energy prices in the Indonesian manufacturing sector

Brucal and Dechezleprêtre (2021[15]), summarised in Chapter 9, look at the Indonesian manufacturing sector, analysing the effect of rising energy prices on energy use, carbon emissions, employment and output. In line with the finding of the French case study, Brucal and Dechezleprêtre (2021[15]) show that a 10% increase in energy prices leads to a decrease of 5.2% in energy use and a reduction of CO_2 emissions by 5.8%. The decrease in employment is much lower, at 0.2%. Rising energy prices also increase the probability of plant exit. However, at the aggregate sectoral level, the analysis shows no statistically significant effect on employment in response to rising energy prices, suggesting that job losses due to plant exit are compensated by job creation in new plants.

Therefore, the results of the case studies looking at the joint environmental and economic effects of environmental policies paint a reassuring picture, with environmental policies reducing emissions without hurting economic performance, in particular employment, at the aggregate level. This is without considering the significant benefits of environmental policies in terms of improved human health and increased welfare, which in cost-benefit analyses typically vastly dominate economic costs (Barde and Pearce, 2013[45]; Rehdanz and Maddison, 2008[46]; Pope and Dockery, 2006[47]; Pruss, 1998[48]). To give just one example, the 1990 Clean Air Act Amendments in the United States are estimated to have induced

USD 100 billion benefits in terms of improved health and other environmental outcomes, for a total estimated compliance cost associated with the adoption of new pollution control technologies well over an order of magnitude smaller, between USD 3 and USD 6 billion (Chestnut and Mills, 2005[49]).

Summing up: What to expect from a 10% increase in relative energy prices?

The results of the studies on economic outcomes summarised in this publication show that more stringent environmental policies do not hurt economic performance significantly on average, with some heterogeneity across firms. Figure 1.13 summarises the magnitudes of the average effects – as estimated across the studies in this book – from a 10% increase in energy prices, which is typical of what most OECD countries have experienced over the 2005-15 decade. The results cover only the manufacturing sector, and are estimated for unilateral increases in energy prices relative to other countries and sectors. The increase in energy prices – which could stem from a price or tax imposed on carbon emissions, for instance – is expected to result in a decline in energy use and carbon intensity of 5% to 10% – a large effect. The effect on energy use and carbon intensity is expected to occur over a similar time horizon as the increase in energy prices, with a short delay of one or two years because firms require time to react to the change. In comparison, the effects on economic outcomes are much smaller, with employment expected to decrease by less than 1% on average. This effect is mostly being driven by energy-intensive firms with low productivity. A 10% increase in energy prices is likely to result in a small decrease of total firm investment and a small increase of around 1.5% of foreign investment by firms. The change in relative energy prices across countries can therefore result in a small shift of investment abroad. Total exports in manufacturing goods are not expected to change as a result of a 10% increase in energy prices. Finally, productivity should slightly increase on average, with highly productive firms expected to observe a small increase in productivity and low-productivity firms expected to experience a small decrease. These effects on economic outcomes are also expected to occur with a short delay of one or two years to the changes in energy prices because firms require time to react and adjust their production processes.

To summarise, a 10% increase in energy prices relative to other countries – recall that industry energy prices increased by 50% between 1995 and 2015 across OECD countries (Figure 1.1) – can deliver substantial environmental benefits through reductions of carbon intensity, while not causing a significant loss of jobs or decline in competitiveness of manufacturing firms. Note that these estimated effects are based on unilateral increases in energy prices, implying that effects on employment and competitiveness would be much smaller if prices were simultaneously raised in other countries. Statements suggesting that carbon pricing would result in substantial job losses and sizable harm to the economy seem to vastly overstate expected economic effects.

Figure 1.13. Expected effects from a 10% increase in energy prices on environmental and economic outcomes in manufacturing sectors

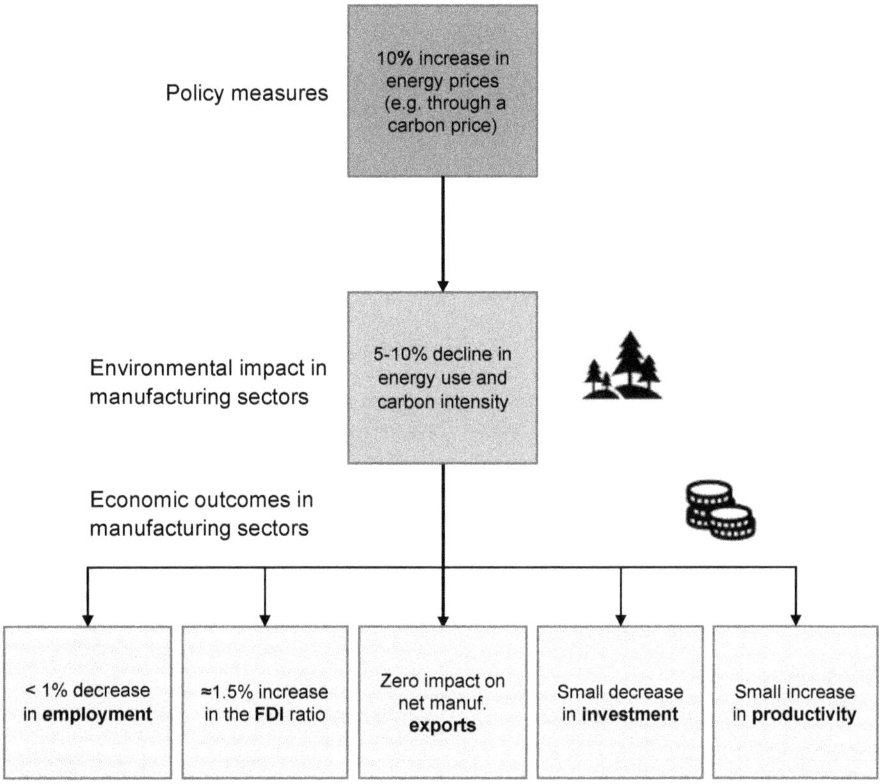

Note: This figure illustrates average expected effects from a 10% increase in industry energy prices on environmental and economic outcomes in manufacturing sectors. It shows effects from across several OECD studies, which cover different samples, time periods and methods. Effects may differ across countries depending on country-specific policy contexts, macro-economic effects and the time horizon.
Source: Authors.

Winners and losers

However, while more stringent environmental policies do not hurt economic performance significantly on average, the results of the studies summarised in this publication show that they also generate winners and losers (see Table 1.1 for a summary of the results). On the one hand, environmental policies entail costs, mainly on high-pollution industries and low-productivity firms: employment (Chapter 3), trade (Chapter 6) and investment outcomes (Chapters 4 and 5) are worsened for pollution-intensive companies, and the productivity of laggard firms is hurt by policy changes (Chapter 2). On the other hand, more stringent environmental policies also have positive effects like improving productivity of frontrunner industries and firms (Chapter 2) or increasing exports in non-pollution-intensive industries (Chapter 6). Overall, the small negative effects seem transitory and environmental policies mainly trigger a reallocation of factors from high- to low-emission industries. Therefore, the evidence summarised in this publication supports both the Porter Hypothesis (environmental policies can increase productivity) and the Pollution Haven hypothesis (environmental policies can increase outward FDI and imports of high-pollution products). It should, however, be kept in mind that the size of the estimated effects is small and that beneficial effects on the environment and human health are not even accounted for.

Table 1.1. Summary of empirical evidence showing the heterogeneity of economic outcomes from a tightening of environmental regulation in manufacturing sectors

Average economic outcomes from tightening of environmental regulation	Firm level		Industry level	
Productivity in manufacturing	High productivity firms	Low productivity firms	High productivity industries	Low productivity industries
	Increase	Decrease	Increase	No effect
Employment in manufacturing	Low productivity, energy-intensive	Others	Energy- intensive	Non-energy-intensive
	Decrease	Increase	Decrease	No effect
Total investment in manufacturing	Energy-intensive listed firms	Non-energy-intensive listed firms	Energy-intensive industries (listed firms)	Non-energy-intensive industries (listed firms)
	Increase	Decrease	Increase	Decrease
FDI in manufacturing	Domestic investment of listed firms	Foreign investment of listed firms	Domestic investment of industries (listed firms)	Foreign investment of industries (listed firms)
	Decrease	Increase	Decrease	Increase
Exports in manufactured goods	/		Pollution-intensive industries	Non-pollution intensive industries
			Decrease	Increase

Source: Authors.

Economy-friendly environmental policies

Implementation of stringent environmental policies remains politically difficult because small but highly localised economic harm (e.g. in terms of employment or competitiveness losses) can generate strong opposition to dealing with environmental issues. Therefore, from both efficiency and political standpoints, it is important to design environmental policies in a way that underpins their positive net effects on the economy without sacrificing their impact on the environment. While a complete treatment of these issues is beyond the scope of this publication, two areas deserve to be mentioned: the choice of environmental policy instrument and the packaging of environmental and other policies.

Appropriate policy design can underpin the economic benefits of environmental policies

Market-based environmental policy instruments, which emit price signals (e.g. taxes, cap and trade systems), are generally considered to be more cost-effective than non-market instruments (e.g. bans, technology standards) (De Serres, Murtin and Nicoletti, 2010[29]). The use of these instruments can therefore be expected to boost the positive effects of environmental policies on firm performance and limit any detrimental impacts. This is mainly because, under a market-based mechanism, firms have more flexibility in choosing the technology and timing of adjustment, compared to technology standards, which tend to be more rigid. Indeed, policy flexibility is one of the key components for a competitiveness-enhancing environmental policy according to Porter and van der Linde (1995[18]).

The results of Albrizio, Koźluk and Zipperer (2017[8]) lend support for the cost-efficiency argument in favour of market-based instruments. They separately assess the impact of market and non-market based instruments on productivity. The firm-level analysis suggests that increases in environmental stringency obtained with market-based instruments may enhance productivity growth of the frontrunners and leave those at the bottom of the productivity distribution almost unaffected (Figure 1.14.), while some evidence suggests that non-market based instruments may slow down productivity growth of laggard firms and do not benefit the productivity of frontrunner firms. However, further empirical work on the differences between market-based and non-market based instruments is needed. Non-market based instruments have, for example, the benefit of being administratively easier and cheaper to implement. They can achieve emission reductions relatively quickly and may even encourage innovation if the technology standard prohibits the use of a specific technology rather than requiring firms to use a specific technology (Klemetsen, Bye and Raknerud, 2013[50]).

In short, compared with other instruments, market-based environmental policies are found to enhance positive effects on the economy, while lowering the negative ones. The case study of the effect of the largest market-based environmental policy in the world, the European Union Emissions Trading System, on economic outcomes (Dechezleprêtre, Nachtigall and Venmans (2018[13]), summarised in Chapter 7) provides additional evidence on the potential benefits of using a market-based policy approach.

Figure 1.14. Market-based policies enhance the positive effects and lower the negative ones

Effects of an increase in market and non-market based components of EPS on firm-level multifactor productivity growth

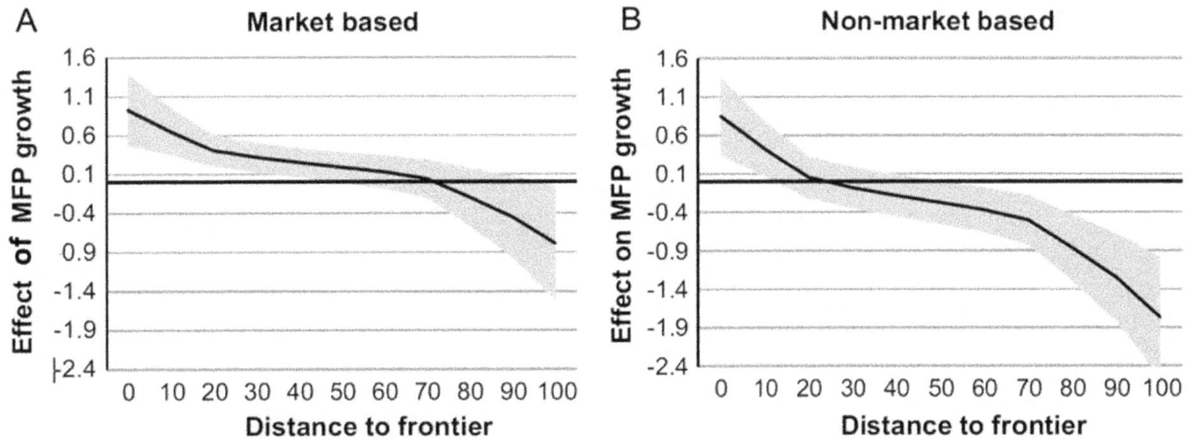

Note: The solid line shows the marginal effect of a one-point tightening of firm-level environmental policy stringency. The grey areas represent the 95% confidence intervals. The horizontal axis represents the distance from the productivity frontier, where 0 represents the firms that are on the frontier, 100 represents the firms furthest from the frontier. Panel A shows the effect of market-based environmental policies, Panel B shows the effect of non-market based policies.
Source: Albrizio, Koźluk and Zipperer (2017[8]).

More stringent environmental policies do not have to come with an increased regulatory burden

Related evidence, based on the OECD indicator of Design and Evaluation of Environmental Policies (DEEP) (Box 1.4), suggests that more stringent environmental policies (as measured by the EPS indicator) need not be associated with heavier burdens on the economy. Plotting the DEEP indicator against the

OECD indicator of environmental policy stringency (EPS) suggests that, depending on the choice of policy instrument, highly stringent policies can be achieved without burdening the economy with restrictions on firm entry and competition (Figure 1.15). For example, countries such as the Netherlands, Switzerland and Austria were able to implement stringent environmental policies while putting relatively little burden on market dynamism.

Figure 1.15. Stringent environmental policies need not put a burden on the economy

EPS vs DEEP indicators

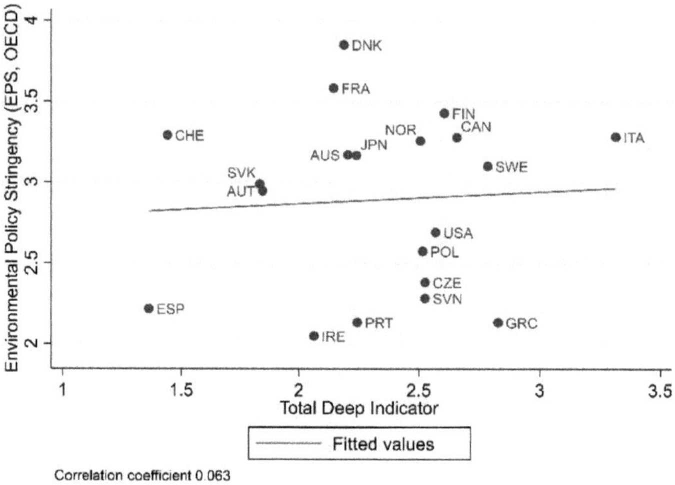

Note: The figure shows the lack of relationship between the stringency of policies and the restrictions they put on the economy in terms of entry and competition. The stringency is measured on the horizontal axis, by the EPS indicator, the burden is measured on the vertical axis, by the DEEP indicator (Box 1.4).
Source: Berestycki and Dechezleprêtre (2020[51]).

Box 1.4. The OECD indicator of Design and Evaluation of Environmental Policies (DEEP)

OECD experience shows that poorly-designed product market regulations can create barriers for entry and competition, which slows economic growth (Bourlès et al., 2013[52]). Similarly, some design and implementation features of environmental policies can burden entry and competition, which could hamper growth. Building upon Koźluk (2014[53]), Berestycki and Dechezleprêtre (2020[51]) construct an indicator of the "Design and Evaluation of Environmental Policies" (DEEP), [13] which is composed of two broad parts: the current administrative burdens and impediments to competition, and the evaluation of past and future environmental policy effects on the economy (Figure 1.16).

Specifically, the first half of the survey, which includes 25 questions, measures the first component: the additional administrative burdens and impediments to competition implied by environmental regulations. For example, the questions ask about the ease of finding information or making an application of new business, or whether the incumbents face different regulations than new entrants. The second half measures the second component: evaluation of new and existing policies. For example, whether an evaluation of new policies takes place involving stakeholders, and what economic effects are evaluated of a new or current policy. Each answer is assigned a score between 0 and 1. The DEEP indicator, similarl to the EPS, runs from 0 to 6, where 6 indicates the highest burdens on the economy. The information collected is primarily *de jure*, reflecting the legal and procedural requirements rather than the actual performance of the administration. The indicator is available for the years 2013 and 2018.

Figure 1.16. Structure of the Design and Evaluation of Environmental Policies (DEEP) indicator

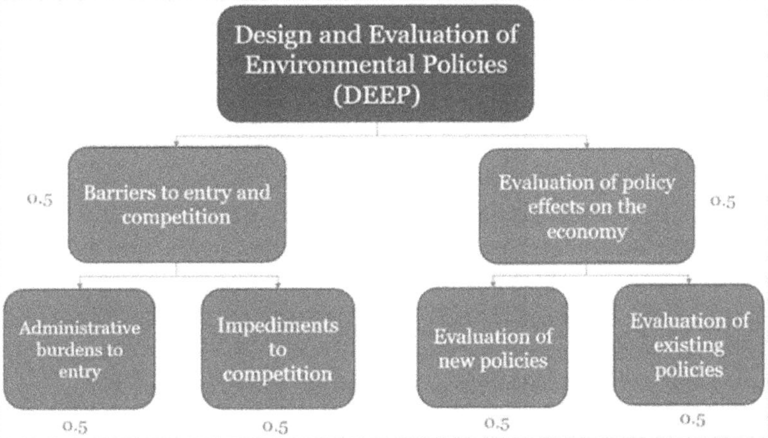

Source: Berestycki and Dechezleprêtre (2020[51]).

Policy packaging could help increase public acceptance of tighter environmental policies

The empirical evidence in this volume shows that past environmental policies have had relatively small effects on economic outcomes. Extrapolating past evidence into the future would therefore suggest that concerns about well-designed policies having large negative impacts on the economy might be exaggerated. While this is encouraging for policy-making, achieving and sustaining public support for such measures can still be challenging. Public support is, however, particularly important for policies on issues such as climate change, which require stable and ambitious measures over multiple decades. Policy packaging to ease such concerns can play an important role and facilitate the political feasibility of environmental policies. Moreover, good packaging could help absorb localised but undesirable economic effects of the transition towards a greener growth path, e.g. in energy-intensive or dirty industries or for laggard firms.

The effect of environmental policies on employment is one of the most politically sensitive aspects. The empirical results suggest that total manufacturing employment is barely affected but some jobs are reallocated across sectors, from the more to the less polluting ones. Since easing reallocation is important to speed up job transitions, especially in the most vulnerable sectors, having effective active labour market policies in place (such as facilitating job search, enhancing skills, life-long training and education) could ease the transition to a cleaner economy, much in the same way as these policies are needed to support other kinds of structural adjustments (OECD, 2011[54]). If job losses are geographically highly clustered in particular regions – for instance in the proximity to fossil fuel reserves – additional specifically targeted labour market policies may be necessary in these regions. This is particularly important if a high share of the local labour force works in such pollution-intensive sectors or if local labour markets cannot absorb a large influx of workers in the short run (OECD, 2012[55]; OECD, 2017[56]).

The use of revenues from environmental policies is a crucial aspect in creating support from the public for ambitious environmental policies (The World Bank, 2018[57]; Carattini, Carvalho and Fankhauser, 2018[58]; Maestre-Andrés, Drews and van den Gergh, 2019[59]; Douenne and Fabre, 2020[60]). While both market-based and non-market based policies can achieve improvements in environmental outcomes, one advantage of market-based policies is that they generate additional public revenues, which can then be reallocated by governments. In order to increase public support, it is often envisaged to target such revenues to achieve the following three objectives, which are discussed in more detail below: first, addressing potential distributional impacts of environmental policies; second, further incentivising environmental innovation through subsidies; third, reducing distortive forms of taxation elsewhere in the economy. Policy makers can thereby design policy packages in a revenue-neutral way, meaning that they do not increase the overall tax burden, dispelling public scepticism that the government simply wants to increase its overall budget through tighter environmental policies.

One approach to recycling revenues, which has received increasing attention more recently, is to recycle parts of the revenues from environmental policies to firms or households through lump-sum payments. Such payments can cushion undesired distributional outcomes and thereby increase public acceptance. It also generates a directly visible benefit from the tax for all households, which can help to sustain public support (Maestre-Andrés, Drews and van den Gergh, 2019[59]; Carattini, Carvalho and Fankhauser, 2018[58]; The Wall Street Journal, 2019[61]). The British Columbia carbon tax provides a prominent example of such a policy design (Harrison, 2013[62]; Murray and Rivers, 2015[63]; Yamazaki, 2017[33]), as does the example of Switzerland's redistribution of parts of their carbon tax revenues.[14]

Another approach to recycle revenues is to fund additional innovation incentives, which can help accelerate the decrease in the costs of abatement technologies. From an economic perspective, it is crucial for environmental policies to provide incentives for technological change because new technologies may substantially reduce the long-run cost of pollution abatement (Harrison, 2013[64]), and innovation is a key component of productivity growth (Aghion and Howitt, 1992[65]). Even though market-based environmental policies already provide incentives for firms to innovate in environmentally-friendly technologies, the revenues from the policy instrument could be used to provide additional financial support for firms investing in such technologies. Innovation support policies, such as public R&D spending, direct grants, R&D tax credits and seed funding could help to provide a significant push for productivity and long-run economic growth, thereby also improving the political acceptability of environmental policies.[15]

Other options to recycle revenues include subsidising the adoption of clean alternatives (electric cars, more efficient appliances, etc.), repaying debt or reducing more distortive forms of taxations such as income taxes. Using the revenues from environmental policy to lower such distortive taxes can increase the efficiency of the economy, while being revenue-neutral. In practice this can be difficult to implement because the main purpose of environmental taxation is to reduce the tax base (i.e. pollution) over time. As the revenues from the tax will decline over time, the introduction of additional taxes may be necessary to balance government budgets. These policies may again be distortive. Moreover, it remains unclear if 'double-dividends' from a reduction of income taxes are actually obtained in practice due to "tax-interaction" effects with other forms of distortive taxation[16] (Aldy et al., 2010[66]). Lastly, using the tax revenue to lower other forms of taxation can reduce the visibility of the revenue use, which weakens the political acceptance compared to alternative approaches (see De Serres, Murtin and Nicoletti (2010[29]) and Maestre-Andrés, Drews and van den Gergh (2019[59]) for comprehensive discussions).

Notes

[1] The OECD's Environmental Policy Stringency (EPS) index aggregates market based and non-market based environmental policies at the country-level over time. The score assigns values from 0 (lowest) to 6 (highest). A higher value indicates more stringent policies. The EPS mainly measures the stringency of energy, air pollution and climate change policies on the country-level, mainly upstream.

[2] Energy prices in this book always refer to industry energy prices. These may be different from energy prices paid by households.

3 Increases in energy prices from taxation allow governments to raise revenue that can be used to compensate disproportionally affected firms. Cross-country information on the share of tax induced versus non-tax induced changes in energy prices do not exist.

4 A separate literature analyses the impacts of environmental policies on households (e.g. Oueslati et al. (2016[73])) which is not covered in this book. For an overview of the related literature on ex-ante modelling work see, for example, Chateau, Bibas and Lanzi (2018[22]) and Chateau, Dellink and Lanzi (2014[74]).

[5] A USD 50/tonne of CO_2 price on carbon emissions is the level generally agreed upon in order to limit further global warming and reach the objectives of the Paris Agreement (see for instance Nordhaus (2017[67]); Dietz et al. (2018[68]); Pindyck (2019[69])).

[6] Global trends in oil prices affect overall energy price levels. It is relevant to note that oil prices in 2020 are lower than in 2014. The latest available data for comprehensive cross-country energy prices that account for important sectoral variation is available for 2014.

[7] To obtain the expected energy price levels, the current country-specific carbon intensity of energy provision is multiplied by the respective carbon price (i.e. USD 50 per tonne of CO_2). To obtain percentage changes, the value of the expected energy price level is compared to the energy price levels in 2014. The overall percentage change is converted to annual percentage changes for the period 2020-30, based on the assumption that the carbon price is introduced gradually from 2020 until 2030 by annual incremental adjustments to reach the respective carbon price in 2030. Expected changes are calculated with respect to 2014 energy price levels using the variable VEPL_MER from the dataset of (Sato et al., 2019[5]). These data incorporate a country-specific fuel mix and therefore country-specific carbon intensities of the overall energy provision.

[8] This is assuming that firm cannot pass on the full costs of the policy.

[9] In the short-run it is also possible that investments lower productivity because firms may need to raise capital, which can mechanically reduce multifactor- or capital productivity.

[10] The analysis by (Albrizio, Koźluk and Zipperer, 2017[8]) (Chapter 2) uses an interaction of the EPS with sector-level pollution intensity, thereby making the EPS sector-specific.

[11] These results are in line with other research that provides direct (Yang, Tseng and Chen, 2012[70]) or indirect (Hamamoto, 2006[71]) evidence that environmental policy enhances industry productivity.

[12] International production, trade and investment are increasingly organised within so-called global value chains where the different stages of the production process are located across different countries. As a result, trade in intermediate goods is no longer proportional to trade in final goods. Trade in value added (TiVA) data can trace back the value added of each country and industry to a final product.

[13] The DEEP indicator was previously called the indicator of Burdens on the Economy due to Environmental Policies.

[14] Recycling revenues lump-sum can help increase the acceptance of policies. However, from an economic efficiency perspective reducing other distortive taxation may be preferable. The revenue recycling prevents that the revenues are used to make the overall tax system more efficient.

[15] Innovation support policies (also know as tax preferences) need to be designed in a way that avoid pitfalls such as technology lock-in into specific technologies that are decided upon by governments, rebound effects that may increase the overall harm to the environment from increased consumption, and windfall gains to firms that would have innovated in a technology also without a subsidy (Greene and Braathen, 2014[75]).

[16] Double-dividends may occur when using environmental tax revenue to lower distortive forms of taxation (e.g. income, payroll or sales tax). The underlying idea is that such an environmental tax design would reduce environmental pollution and at the same time improve economic efficiency. However, environmental taxation also raise costs to firms, which in combination with existing distortionary taxation may create additional inefficiencies and costs to society. This effect may reduce or offset potential double-dividend effects (for a detailed review see, for example, Goulder (2013[72]).

References

Aghion, P. and P. Howitt (1992), "A Model of Growth through Creative Destruction", *Econometrica*, Vol. 60/2, pp. 323-351, https://ideas.repec.org/a/ecm/emetrp/v60y1992i2p323-51.html (accessed on 25 February 2019). [65]

Agrawala, S., D. Dussaux and N. Monti (2020), "What policies for greening the crisis response and economic recovery?: Lessons learned from past green stimulus measures and implications for the COVID-19 crisis", *OECD Environment Working Papers*, No. 164, OECD Publishing, Paris, https://dx.doi.org/10.1787/c50f186f-en. [4]

Albrizio, S., T. Koźluk and V. Zipperer (2017), "Environmental policies and productivity growth: Evidence across industries and firms", *Journal of Environmental Econonics and Management*, Vol. 81, pp. 209-226. [8]

Aldy, J. et al. (2010), "Designing Climate Mitigation Policy", *Journal of Economic Literature*, Vol. 48/4, pp. 903-934, http://dx.doi.org/10.1257/jel.48.4.903. [66]

Aldy, J. and W. Pizer (2015), "The Competitiveness Impacts of Climate Change Mitigation Policies", *Journal of the Association of Environmental and Resource Economists*, Vol. 2/4, pp. 565-595, http://dx.doi.org/10.1086/683305. [27]

Andrews, D., M. McGowan and V. Millot (2017), "Confronting the zombies: Policies for Productivity Revival", *OECD Economic Policy Papers* 21, pp. 1-35. [30]

Arntz, M., T. Gregory and U. Zierahn (2016), "The risk of automation for jobs in OECD countries", *OECD Social, Employment and Migration Working Papers*, No. 189, OECD, Paris, https://doi.org/10.1787/5jlz9h56dvq7-en (accessed on 8 January 2019). [35]

Barde, J. and D. Pearce (2013), *Valuing the Environment*, Routledge. [45]

Berestycki, C. and A. Dechezleprêtre (2020), "Assessing the efficiency of environmental policy design and evaluation: Results from a 2018 cross-country survey", *OECD Economics Department Working Papers*, No. 1611, OECD Publishing, Paris, https://dx.doi.org/10.1787/482f8fbe-en. [51]

Botta, E. and T. Koźluk (2014), "Measuring environmental policy stringency in OECD countries", *Economics Department Working Papers*, No. 1177, OECD, Paris, https://doi.org/10.1787/5jxrjnc45gvg-en (accessed on 17 January 2019). [28]

Bourlès, R. et al. (2013), "Do Product Market Regulations In Upstream Sectors Curb Productivity Growth? Panel Data Evidence For OECD Countries", *Review of Economics and Statistics*, Vol. 95/5, pp. 1750-1768, http://dx.doi.org/10.1162/REST_a_00338. [52]

Branger, F., P. Quirion and J. Chevallier (2017), "Carbon Leakage and Competitiveness of Cement and Steel Industries Under the EU ETS: Much Ado About Nothing", *The Energy Journal*, Vol. 37/3, http://dx.doi.org/10.5547/01956574.37.3.fbra. [38]

Brucal, A. and A. Dechezleprêtre (2021), "Assessing the impact of energy prices on plant-level environmental and economic performance: Evidence from Indonesian manufacturers", *OECD Environment Working Papers*, No. 170, OECD Publishing, Paris, https://dx.doi.org/10.1787/9ec54222-en. [15]

Carattini, S., M. Carvalho and S. Fankhauser (2018), "Overcoming public resistance to carbon taxes", *WIRES Climate Change*, Vol. 9/5, https://doi.org/10.1002/wcc.531. [58]

Chateau, J., R. Bibas and E. Lanzi (2018), "Impacts of Green Growth Policies on Labour Markets and Wage Income Distribution: A General Equilibrium Application to Climate and Energy Policies", *OECD Environment Working Papers*, No. 137, OECD Publishing, Paris, https://dx.doi.org/10.1787/ea3696f4-en. [22]

Château, J., R. Dellink and E. Lanzi (2014), "An Overview of the OECD ENV-Linkages Model: Version 3", *OECD Environment Working Papers*, No. 65, OECD Publishing, Paris, https://dx.doi.org/10.1787/5jz2qck2b2vd-en. [74]

Chestnut, L. and D. Mills (2005), "A fresh look at the benefits and costs of the US acid rain program", *Journal of Environmental Management*, Vol. 77/3, pp. 252-266, https://doi.org/10.1016/j.jenvman.2005.05.014. [49]

De Serres, A., F. Murtin and G. Nicoletti (2010), "A framework for assessing green growth policies", *Economics Department Working Papes*, No. 774, OECD, Paris, https://www.oecd-ilibrary.org/content/workingpaper/5kmfj2xvcmkf-en (accessed on 22 January 2019). [29]

Dechenes, O. (2011), "Climate policy and labor markets", in Fullerton, D. and C. Wolfram (eds.), *The design and implementation of US climate policy*, University of Chicago Press, Chicago, http://www.nber.org/chapters/c12150.pdf (accessed on 25 January 2019). [32]

Dechezleprêtre, A. et al. (2019), "Do environmental and economic performance go together? A review of micro-level empirical evidence from the past decade or so", *International Review of Environmental and Resource Economics*, Vol. 13, pp. 1-118, http://dx.doi.org/10.1561/101.00000106. [31]

Dechezleprêtre, A., D. Nachtigall and B. Stadler (2020), "The effect of energy prices and environmental policy stringency on manufacturing employment in OECD countries: Sector- and firm-level evidence", *OECD Economics Department Working Papers*, No. 1625, OECD Publishing, Paris, https://dx.doi.org/10.1787/899eb13f-en. [9]

Dechezleprêtre, A., D. Nachtigall and F. Venmans (2018), "The joint impact of the European Union emissions trading system on carbon emissions and economic performance", *OECD Economics Department Working Papers*, No. 1515, OECD Publishing, Paris, https://dx.doi.org/10.1787/4819b016-en. [13]

Dechezleprêtre, A. and M. Sato (2017), "The impacts of environmental regulations on competitiveness", *Review of Environmental Economics and Policy*, pp. 183-206, https://doi.org/10.1093/reep/rex013. [34]

Dietz, S. et al. (2018), "The Economics of 1.5°C Climate Change", *Annual Review of Environment and Resources*, Vol. 43, pp. 455-480. [68]

Dlugosch, D. and T. Koźluk (2017), "Energy prices, environmental policies and investment - evidence from listed firms", *OECD Economics Department Working Papers*, Vol. 1378, https://doi.org/10.1787/ef6c01c6-en. [10]

Douenne, T. and A. Fabre (2020), "French attitudes on climate change, carbon taxation and other climate policies", *Ecological Economics*, Vol. 169, http://dx.doi.org/10.1016/j.ecolecon.2019.106496. [60]

Dussaux, D. (2020), "The joint effects of energy prices and carbon taxes on environmental and economic performance: Evidence from the French manufacturing sector", *OECD Environment Working Papers*, No. 154, OECD Publishing, Paris, https://dx.doi.org/10.1787/b84b1b7d-en. [14]

Fankhauser, S., F. Sehhleier and N. Stern (2008), "Climate change, innovation and jobs", *Climate Policy*, Vol. 8/4, pp. 421-429, http://dx.doi.org/doi:10.3763/cpol.2008.0513. [23]

Garsous, G., T. Koźluk and D. Dlugosch (2020), "Do energy prices drive outwards FDI? Evidence from a sample of listed firms", *The Energy Journal*, Vol. 41/3, http://dx.doi.org/doi:10.5547/01956574.41.3.ggar. [11]

Goulder, L. (2013), "Climate change policy's interactions with the tax system", *Energy Economics*, Vol. 40/S3-S11, https://doi.org/10.1016/j.eneco.2013.09.017. [72]

Greene, J. and N. Braathen (2014), "Tax Preferences for Environmental Goals: Use, Limitations and Preferred Practices", *OECD Environment Working Papers*, No. 71, OECD Publishing, Paris, https://dx.doi.org/10.1787/5jxwrr4hkd6l-en. [75]

Guarini, G. (2020), "The Macroeonomic Impact of the Porter Hypothesis: Sustainability and Environmental Policies in a Post-Keynesian Model", *Review of Political Economy*, Vol. 32/1, pp. 30-48, https://doi.org/10.1080/09538259.2020.1748308. [20]

Hamamoto, M. (2006), "Environmental regulation and the productivity of Japanese manufacturing industries", *Resource and energy economics*, Vol. 28/4, pp. 299-312, https://doi.org/10.1016/j.reseneeco.2005.11.001. [71]

Harrison, K. (2013), "The Political Economy of British Columbia's Carbon Tax", *OECD Environment Working Papers*, No. 63, OECD Publishing, Paris, https://dx.doi.org/10.1787/5k3z04gkkhkg-en. [62]

Harrison, K. (2013), "The Political Economy of British Columbia's Carbon Tax", *OECD Environment Working Papers*, No. 63, OECD Publishing, Paris, https://dx.doi.org/10.1787/5k3z04gkkhkg-en. [64]

Kahn, M. and E. Mansur (2013), "Do local energy prices and regulation affect the geographic concentration of employment?", *Journal of Public Economics*, Vol. 101, pp. 105-114, https://doi.org/10.1016/j.jpubeco.2013.03.002. [24]

Klemetsen, M., B. Bye and A. Raknerud (2013), "Can non-market regulations spur innovations in environmental technologies - A study on firm level patenting", *Statistics Norway Research Department Working Paper*, Vol. 754, https://www.ssb.no/en/forskning/discussion-papers/_attachment/140478. [50]

Klemetsen, M., K. Rosendahl and A. Jakobsen (2020), "The impacts of the EU ETS on Norwegian Plants' Environmental and Economic Performance", *Climate Change Economics*, Vol. 11/1, https://doi.org/10.1142/S2010007820500062. [44]

Koźluk, T. (2014), "The Indicators of the Economic Burdens of Environmental Policy Design: Results from the OECD Questionnaire", *OECD Economic Department Working Papers*, No. 1178, OECD, Paris, http://search.proquest.com/openview/6148626dc8861b21841e152fb2d33e98/1?pq-origsite=gscholar&cbl=54478 (accessed on 25 January 2019). [53]

Koźluk, T. and C. Timiliotis (2016), "Do Environmental Policies affect Global Value Chains? A new perspective on the pollution haven hypothesis", *Economics Department Working Papers*, No. ECO/WKP(2016)6, OECD, Paris. [12]

Laing, T. et al. (2014), "The effects and side-effects of the EU emissions trading scheme", *WIRES Climate Change*, https://doi.org/10.1002/wcc.283. [41]

Levinson, A. (2010), "Offshoring pollution: Is the United States Increasingly Importing Polluting Goods?", *Review of Environmental Economics and Policy*, Vol. 4/1, pp. 63-83, https://doi.org/10.1093/reep/rep017. [40]

Levinson, A. and M. Taylor (2008), "Unmasking the pollution haven effect", *International Economic Review*, Vol. 49/1, pp. 223-254, http://dx.doi.org/10.1111/j.1468-2354.2008.00478.x. [37]

Maestre-Andrés, S., S. Drews and J. van den Gergh (2019), "Perceived fairness and public acceptability of carbon pricing: a review of the literature", *Climate Policy*, Vol. 19/9, pp. 1186-1204, https://doi.org/10.1080/14693062.2019.1639490. [59]

McGuire, M. (1982), "Regulation, factor rewards, and international trade", *Journal of Public Economics*, Vol. 17/3, https://www.sciencedirect.com/science/article/pii/004727278290069X (accessed on 17 January 2019). [16]

Morgenstern, R., W. Pizer and J. Shih (2002), "Jobs versus the environment: An industry-level perspective", *Journal of Environmental Economics and Management*, Vol. 43/3, pp. 412-436, https://doi.org/10.1006/jeem.2001.1191. [21]

Murray, B. and N. Rivers (2015), "British Columbia's revenue-neutral carbon tax: A review of the latest "grand experiment" in environmental policy", *Energy Policy*, https://www.sciencedirect.com/science/article/pii/S0301421515300550. [63]

Nordhaus, W. (2017), "Revisiting the social cost of carbon", *PNAS*, Vol. 114/7, pp. 1518-1523, https://doi.org/10.1073/pnas.1609244114. [67]

OECD (2020), *Building back better: A sustainable, resilient recovery after COVID-19*, OECD Publishing, Paris, http://www.oecd.org/coronavirus/policy-responses/building-back-better-a-sustainable-resilient-recovery-after-covid-19-52b869f5/. [2]

OECD (2020), *COVID-19 and the low-carbon transition. Impacts and possible policy response*, OECD Publishing, Paris, http://www.oecd.org/coronavirus/policy-responses/covid-19-and-the-low-carbon-transition-impacts-and-possible-policy-responses-749738fc/. [1]

OECD (2020), *OECD Economic Outlook, Volume 2020 Issue 1*, OECD Publishing, Paris, https://dx.doi.org/10.1787/0d1d1e2e-en. [3]

OECD (2019), *GDP volume - annual growth rate*, https://stats.oecd.org/index.aspx?queryid=60703. [6]

OECD (2019), *Unemployment rate*, https://dx.doi.org/10.1787/997c8750-en (accessed on 17 January 2019). [7]

OECD (2017), *Employment Implications of Green Growth: Linking jobs, growth, and green policies*, OECD Publishing, Paris, https://www.oecd.org/environment/Employment-Implications-of-Green-Growth-OECD-Report-G7-Environment-Ministers.pdf. [56]

OECD (2012), *OECD Employment Outlook 2012*, OECD Publishing, Paris, https://dx.doi.org/10.1787/empl_outlook-2012-en. [55]

OECD (2011), *Towards Green Growth*, OECD Green Growth Studies, OECD Publishing, Paris, https://dx.doi.org/10.1787/9789264111318-en. [54]

Oueslati, W. et al. (2016), "Exploring the relationship between environmentally related taxes and inequality in income sources", *OECD Environment Working Papers, No. 100*, https://doi.org/10.1787/19970900. [73]

Petrick, S. and U. Wagner (2014), "The impact of carbon trading on industry: Evidence from German manufacturing (RMS)", *Kiel Working Paper*, Vol. No. 1912, https://www.econstor.eu/handle/10419/94357. [43]

Pindyck, R. (2019), "The social cost of carbon revisited", *Journal of Environmental Economics and Management*, Vol. 94, pp. 140-160. [69]

Pope, C. and D. Dockery (2006), "Health Effects of fine particulate air pollution: lines that connect", *Journal of the Air & Waste Management Association*, Vol. 56/6, pp. 709-742, https://doi.org/10.1080/10473289.2006.10464485. [47]

Porter, M. (1991), "America's green strategy", *Scientific American*, https://books.google.fr/books?hl=fr&lr=&id=i7UDHlOGfPEC&oi=fnd&pg=PA33&dq=porter+americas+green+strategy&ots=AN4z5Eq9YG&sig=GXJp7n_hiAcLtkpn-sCpUDK1UzU (accessed on 17 January 2019). [17]

Porter, M. and C. van der Linde (1995), "Toward a New Conception of the Environment-Competitiveness Relationship", *Journal of Economic Perspectives*, Vol. 9/4, pp. 97-118, http://dx.doi.org/10.1257/jep.9.4.97. [18]

Pruss, A. (1998), "Review of epidemiological studies on health effects from exposure to recreational water", *International Journal of Epidemiology*, Vol. 27/1, pp. 1-9, https://pubmed.ncbi.nlm.nih.gov/9563686/. [48]

Qiu, L., M. Zhou and X. Wei (2018), "Regulation, innovation, and firm selection: The porter hypothesis under monopolistic competition", *Journal of Environmental Economics and Management*, Vol. 92, pp. 638-658, https://doi.org/10.1016/j.jeem.2017.08.012. [19]

Rehdanz, K. and D. Maddison (2008), "Local environmental quality and life-satisfaction in Germany", *Ecological Economics*, Vol. 64/4, pp. 787-797, https://doi.org/10.1016/j.ecolecon.2007.04.016. [46]

Sato, M. and A. Dechezleprêtre (2015), "Asymmetric industrial energy prices and international trade", *Energy Economics*, Vol. 52, pp. S130-S141, http://dx.doi.org/10.1016/J.ENECO.2015.08.020. [39]

Sato, M. et al. (2019), "International and sectoral variation in industry energy prices 1995-2015", *Energy Economics*, Vol. 78, pp. 235-258. [5]

Sauvage, J. (2014), "The Stringency of Environmental Regulations and Trade in Environmental Goods", *OECD Trade and Environment Working Papers*, No. 2014/3, OECD, Paris, http://search.proquest.com/openview/6148626dc8861b2176bc42ccf45cf5ce/1?pq-origsite=gscholar&cbl=54500 (accessed on 25 January 2019). [36]

The Wall Street Journal (2019), *Economists' statement on carbon dividends*, https://www.wsj.com/articles/economists-statement-on-carbon-dividends-11547682910#:~:text=A%20carbon%20tax%20should%20increase,and%20large%2Dscale%20infrastructure%20development. [61]

The World Bank (2018), *Guide to Communicating Carbon Pricing*, https://openknowledge.worldbank.org/bitstream/handle/10986/30921/132534-WP-WBFINALonline.pdf?sequence=9&isAllowed=y. [57]

Wagner, U. et al. (2014), "The Causal Effects of the European Union Emissions Trading Scheme: Evidence from French Manufacturing Plants", *Working Paper*, http://conference.iza.org/conference_files/EnvEmpl2014/martin_r7617.pdf. [42]

Xepapadeas, A. and A. de Zeeuw (1998), "Environmental Policy and Competitiveness: The Porter Hypothesis and the Composition of Capital", *Journal of Environmental Economics and Management*, pp. 165-182, https://doi.org/10.1006/jeem.1998.1061. [25]

Xing, Y. and C. Kolstad (2002), "Do Lax Environmental Regulations Attract Foreign Investment?", *Environmental and Resource Economics*, Vol. 21, pp. 1-22, https://doi.org/10.1023/A:1014537013353. [26]

Yamazaki, A. (2017), "Jobs and climate policy: Evidence from British Columbia's revenue-neutral carbon tax", *Journal of Environmental Economics and Management*, Vol. 83, pp. 197-216, http://dx.doi.org/10.1016/J.JEEM.2017.03.003. [33]

Yang, C., Y. Tseng and C. Chen (2012), "Environmental regulations, induced R&D, and productivity: Evidence from Taiwan's manufacturing industries", *Resource and Energy Economics*, Vol. 34/4, pp. 514-532, https://doi.org/10.1016/j.reseneeco.2012.05.001. [70]

2 Productivity growth, environmental policies and the Porter Hypothesis

The link between environmental policies and productivity growth is the focus of this chapter.[1] New regulations often impose additional costs on firms, thereby reducing their productivity. However, new regulations might also trigger productivity increases through a redesign of production processes or a reallocation of resources within firms. This hypothesis is known as the Porter Hypothesis and has been the subject of a number of empirical studies. However, the evidence is inconclusive so far, especially at the cross-country level as a comparable measure of environmental policy stringency was missing to date. This study uses the OECD EPS indicator, a cross-country indicator for environmental policy stringency, to provide new evidence on the Porter Hypothesis. Using an extended neo-Schumpeterian productivity model, it looks at productivity developments at the industry and firm level of 17 OECD countries over the period 1990 to 2009. The results suggest that better environmental protection is associated with a short-term increase in industry-level productivity growth in countries that are considered to be at the technology frontier. The firm-level analysis shows that only the most productive firms are able to reap productivity gains while the least productive ones face a productivity decline.

Background

Environmental policies affect firms' economic performance

Over the past decades, governments implemented a range of environmental policies with the objective of protecting the environment and human health. These policies can broadly be differentiated between policies based on price mechanisms (market-based instruments) or command-and-control policies which enforce environmental standards (non-market based instruments). These policies inevitably change production processes, resource allocation within and among firms, capital investment and innovation incentives, which all affect the economic performance of firms.

Productivity increases at the firm level are possible due to previously overlooked potential gains

Environmental policies pose a burden on firms through shifting the use of resources from 'productive uses' to pollution abatement, thereby potentially lowering the productivity of firms. However, the Porter Hypothesis (PH) suggests that environmental policies might instead raise the productivity of firms. As suggested by Porter and van der Linde (1995[1]; Porter, 1991[2]), firms might see an increase of productivity through within-firm resource reallocation, efficiency improvements, a re-design of production processes or innovation. Three versions of the so-called Porter Hypothesis have been put forward (Jaffe and Palmer, 1997[3]): the weak version suggests that environmental policies stimulate innovation, the strong version states that environmental policies lead to higher overall productivity of firms, and the narrow version claims that innovation and productivity gains are more likely under adequate policies, i.e. market-based policies. This study focuses on the strong and narrow version of the Porter Hypothesis.

An industry-level analysis allows to take reallocation across firms into account

At the industry level, effects of environmental policies on industry productivity might differ from effects at the firm level, because of potential factor reallocation across firms within an industry: some firms might exit the market because they are unable to cope with the new regulation, new firms might enter with disruptive technologies, and production might be shifted away from less productive toward more productive firms. If, additionally, environmental policies were to affect market barriers to entry or trade flows, competitive pressure in the market could decline, potentially leading to a decrease in productivity.

Empirical evidence is inconclusive so far

The empirical evidence on the Porter Hypothesis has been inconclusive so far. Studies mainly focus on the strong version (productivity effect) and weak version (innovation effect) and results vary across the level of analysis (country, industry, firm level) (see Cohen and Tubb, (2017[4])2017; Koźluk and Zipperer, (2014[5]); and Ambec et al. (2013[6]), for detailed overviews). The studies often lack a cross-country dimension because comparable measures of environmental policies were not readily available. At the industry level, the literature is still inconclusive about the significance and the direction of the effect. Early work indicated a negative effect but was often characterised by context-specific set-ups and suffered from identification problems (Gray, 1987[7]; Barbera and McConnell, 1990[8]; Dufour, Lanoie and Patry, 1998[9]). More recent work is often based on longer time series and rather finds positive or no effects (Hamamoto, 2006[10]; Yang, Tseng and Chen, 2012[11]; Lanoie, Patry and Lajeunesse, 2008[12]; Franco and Marin, 2017[13]; Rubashkina, Galeotti and Verdolini, 2015[14]; Alpay, Buccola and Kerkvliet, 2002[15]). At the firm level, recent studies tend to find a negative effect of environmental regulation on productivity (Becker, 2011[16]; Gray and Shadbegian, 2003[17]). However, all of the studies focus on specific industries in a single country setting or very specific regulations, and thus lack generality.

Contribution of this study – first large-scale panel study, combining industry and firm level analysis

This study offers two main contributions to the literature. First, it is the first study to provide cross-country evidence on the strong version of the Porter Hypothesis by using the environmental policy stringency indicator (EPS) recently developed by the OECD (see Box 1.3. in Chapter 1 for details on the EPS indicator; see also Botta and Koźluk (2014[18]). This panel study thus allows a more global view on the Porter Hypothesis than the earlier single-country studies. Second, it is the first analysis of the Porter Hypothesis combining firm- and industry-level results, offering additional insights on the channels at work behind the effects. While the industry-level analysis covers aggregate effects and reallocations among firms, it might suffer from aggregation bias as some firm-level effects might cancel each other out. The firm-level analysis allows for heterogeneous effects among firms but suffers from representativeness bias and has limitations in tracking entry and exit dynamics.

Empirical set-up

An augmented neo-Schumpeterian growth model to analyse productivity effects

A standard neo-Schumpeterian model of multifactor productivity growth is used and augmented with environmental regulation. Multifactor productivity growth is modelled to be driven by a technological catch-up effect, indicating the industries' (or firms') ability to adopt the newest technologies, and a technological pass-through effect, indicating the industries' (or firms') ability to innovate (Acemoglu, Aghion and Zilibotti, 2006[19]; Aghion and Howitt, 2006[20]; Nicoletti and Scarpetta, 2003[21]). Multifactor productivity growth is then modelled to also depend on the country's environmental regulation. Following Bourlès et al. (2013[22]), this regulation is allowed to influence multifactor productivity growth in a heterogeneous way, differing with the industry's/firm's distance to the technological frontier. More technologically advanced industries and firms are assumed to be better capable of adopting new regulations as they are likely to have more (financial) resources to invest into research and development, better access to new technologies, financial markets or managerial capacity.

Heterogeneous industry effects through different exposure to country-level environmental regulation

The effect of environmental policy stringency on multifactor productivity is allowed to vary across industries, depending on their exposure to the regulation. The environmental policy variable (EPS) is measured at the country level. However, depending on the environmental dependence of an industry, the sector might be differently affected by the regulation. Therefore, the EPS variable is interacted with the pre-sample industry's pollution intensity to account for these heterogeneous effects. This approach is common in the literature analysing country-level policies and industry/firm developments and was first proposed by Rajan and Zingales (1998[23]) in the context of work on financial markets.

Empirical model

The empirical model incorporates lagged changes in environmental regulation. Instead of looking at the level of environmental policy stringency, the study focuses on regulatory changes as this is assumed to be a stronger driver for investment decisions by firms, potentially leading to productivity effects. As the effects of environmental policy changes might take time, a moving average of the past three years of changes in EPS is used to account for lagged effects in the adaptation process of firms. The following model is estimated:

$$\Delta \ln MFP_{cit} = \propto_1 + \alpha_2 \frac{1}{3}\sum_{j=1}^{3}(ED_{i\,1987}\Delta EPS_{ct-j}) + \alpha_3 gap_{cit-1}\frac{1}{3}\sum_{j=1}^{3}(ED_{i\,1987}\Delta EPS_{ct-j})$$

$$+\propto_4 gap_{cit-1} + \propto_5 \Delta \ln \widehat{MFP}_{it} + x_{cit}\gamma + \eta_t + \delta_{ci} + \epsilon_{cit}$$

where *c* indexes countries, *t* indexes years and *i* indexes industries (in the industry-level regressions) or firms (in the firm-level regressions). $\Delta \ln MFP_{cit}$ is the multifactor productivity growth for each combination of country *c* and industry/firm *i* at time *t*. ΔEPS_{ct-j} is the change in the country's environmental policy stringency, multiplied with a pre-sample measure for the industry's pollution intensity, $ED_{i\,1987}$ (see Albrizio, Koźluk and Zipperer (2017[24]) for more details). The technology gap allows for catch-up effects and is defined as the distance to the productivity frontier, $gap_{cit-1} = \ln(\frac{\widehat{\mathrm{MFP}}_{\mathrm{I}}}{MFP_{ci}})$. At the industry level, the global technology frontier is defined as the highest productivity growth rate among countries by industry and year (corrected for outliers). At the firm level, the global technology frontier is defined as the average productivity growth of the top-5% firms across countries, by industry and year. $\Delta \ln \widehat{MFP}_{it}$ is the technological pass-through, measured as the growth rate of the leader productivity. The vector x_{cit} contains country and industry-/firm-specific control variables, including the output gap, a dummy for the financial crisis, a common time trend, employment protection legislation, product market regulation, and lagged R&D expenditure over value-added. Further, a time trend η_t is included and country-industry fixed effects δ_{ci} (or alternatively country and industry fixed effects, δ_c and δ_i. Additionally, the firm level analysis controls for the total asset turnover and the firms' size as lagged log number of employees.

Data

The industry level dataset covers 17 OECD countries and 10 manufacturing sectors over the time period 1990-2009. Productivity is calculated with a Cobb-Douglas production function, based on data from the OECD Structural Analysis database (STAN) and the Database Productivity by industry (PDBi).[2] The firm level dataset covers 11 OECD countries and 22 manufacturing sectors over the time period 2000-09. The calculation of productivity data follows Wooldridge (2009[25]), using data from the OECD-ORBIS database developed by Gal (2013[26]) based on data from the Bureau Van Dijk ORBIS dataset. Data on the environmental dependence of industries, measured as pollution-intensity, are taken from the World Bank's IPPS Pollution Intensity and Abatement Cost dataset, and used for the US manufacturing sector in 1987.

Results

Support for the strong version of the Porter Hypothesis at the industry level

At the industry level, tighter environmental policies are found to be associated with a positive short-term effect on productivity growth, in countries that are close to the technological frontier (Table 2.1. , columns 1 and 2). This positive effect diminishes with the distance to the frontier and eventually becomes insignificant. Importantly, however, no industry experiences a decline in productivity growth as environmental policies become tighter. The technological catch-up term, i.e. the coefficient of the gap_{cit-1}variable, is also positive and significant, as is the MFP growth rate of the leader, indicating technological pass-through to lagging industries. In order to evaluate the magnitude of the effect of changes in EPS on industry productivity growth, marginal effects are calculated, taking into account the interaction between EPS and the technological gap of the industry to the productivity frontier. Figure 2.1 (left-hand panel) shows the marginal effects calculated for high-polluting industries for a change in EPS of 0.12 points (which corresponds to the mean in-sample change of the EPS).

Table 2.1. Porter Hypothesis - main estimation results

Dependent variable: MFP growth	Industry-level		Firm-level	
	1	2	3	4
EPS tightening°	0.12***	0.12***	0.34***	0.34***
	(0.02)	(0.03)	(0.08)	(0.09)
Gap * EPS tightening°	-0.15***	-0.16**	-0.15***	-0.18***
	(0.05)	(0.07)	(0.05)	(0.05)
Leader MFP growth	0.12***	0.14***	0.13***	0.16***
	(0.03)	(0.03)	(0.02)	(0.02)
Gap (t-1)	0.088***	0.16***	0.21***	0.28***
	(0.01)	(0.03)	(0.03)	(0.01)
Fixed effects				
Country*Industry	No	Yes	No	Yes
Country	Yes	No	Yes	No
Industry	Yes	No	Yes	No
N	1954	1954	1062460	1062460
Adjusted R^2	0.184	0.117	0.104	0.132

Note: All columns include the control variables discussed above, i.e. the output gap, employment protection legislation, product market regulation, R&D intensity, a crisis dummy and a year trend. The firm-level analysis (column 3 and 4) additionally includes the return on investment, firm size and asset turnover as control variables. Robust standard errors in parentheses and they are clustered at country-industry level; *** denotes statistical significance at the 1% level, ** significance at 5% level, * significance at 10% level. ° denotes the moving average of the EPS change over three-years-lags.

High-productivity firms win, low-productivity firms lose out

At the firm level, the results show a positive coefficient of the environmental policy stringency variable (Table 2.1. , columns 3 and 4). However, when calculating the marginal effect for the distribution of firms, only one fifth of the firms are able to reap productivity gains as Figure 2.1 (right-hand panel) shows. The least productive firms face a statistically significant productivity decline.

Figure 2.1. Marginal effects of increasing environmental policy stringency for high-polluting industries

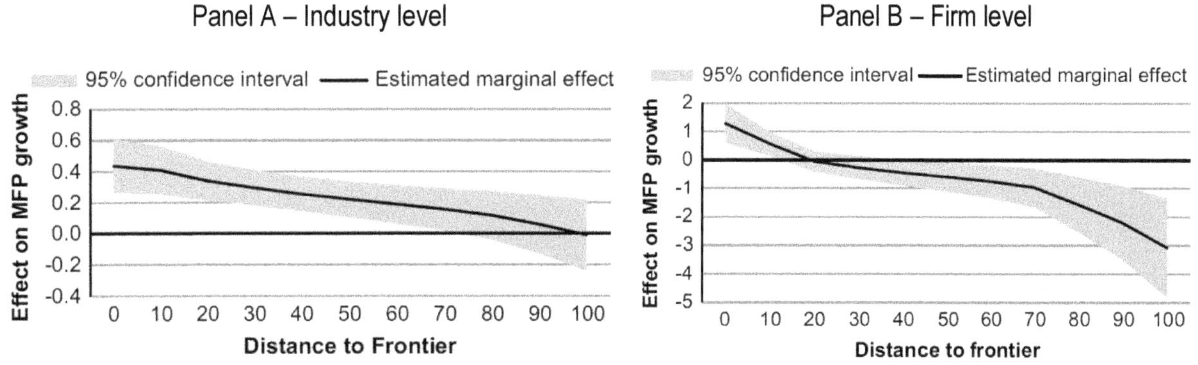

Note: The annual productivity effect of a 0.12 point increase in the environmental policy stringency indicator (equal to the in-sample mean of changes in EPS) is shown for highly polluting industries. Grey bands show 95% confidence interval. The figure shows short-term effects based on the estimation results reported in Table 2.1.

Difference in industry and firm level results are likely driven by exit dynamics

While the positive effect in technologically-advanced industries might be due to a better ability to improve production technologies or a better access to financial markets, it might also result from an aggregation bias. Low-productivity firms might be driven out of the market because they are not able to adapt to the new regulation or firms might outsource emission-intensive production processes. To investigate whether less technologically advanced firms are driven out of the market or reduce their activity, the analysis uses data on the age of firms to proxy the in-sample survival of firms (for a sub-sample of firms for which this data is available). Results show that firm survival is indeed negatively correlated with the distance to the technological frontier, pointing towards a higher exit rate of the least productive firms. This indicates that the difference in industry and firm level results is indeed due to entry and exit dynamics. The most productive firms in the distribution might be more likely to be part of a multinational firm or to trade internationally, and thus have more resources and capacity to adapt to changes in environmental regulations.

The effects are independent of the level of environmental regulation but depend on policy design

The comparative stringency of environmental regulation does not have an influence on the productivity effects observed. By interacting the "change in EPS"-variable with a dummy variable indicating whether the absolute level of EPS is above or below the sample average, the analysis investigates whether a tightening of regulation has a more detrimental effect in countries with high environmental protection compared to countries taking a laxer approach. The results show no significant difference in the effect of high- versus low-regulation countries. A further analysis at the firm level differentiates the design of environmental policies into market-based and non-market based components. In line with the narrow version of the Porter Hypothesis, the results show that market-based policies are more productivity-friendly, in line with economic theory suggesting the greater cost-efficiency of price-based mechanisms.

The results are robust and potential endogeneity concerns are limited

The results of the industry- and firm-level regressions are robust to several checks, including a different definition of the environmental dependence variable, excluding fossil-fuel dependent countries[3] (as the EPS indicator is largely based on upstream regulations), and a re-estimation with a different environmental policy proxy based on a survey of the World Economic Forum which focuses on the enforcement of environmental policies. Endogeneity concerns might arise because of reverse causality or simultaneity, e.g. when poorly performing firms successfully lobby the government not to implement more stringent policies. The nature of the EPS indicator (being based largely on out-of-sample, upstream sectors) makes potential lobbying effects unlikely, while using the lagged variables mitigates simultaneity issues. Testing in a regression framework whether past changes in productivity growth are able to predict changes in the environmental policy variable shows no significant support (see Albrizio, Koźluk and Zipperer (2017[24]) for more details).

Conclusion

Summary of results

The analysis shows some support for the strong version of the Porter Hypothesis. At the industry level, the most technologically advanced country-industry pairs see a positive short-term effect of a tightening of environmental policy on their productivity. This effect declines with the distance to the technological frontier, eventually becoming insignificant for the least productive country-industry pairs. At the firm level, results show that one fifth of the firms – the most productive ones – are able to reap productivity gains. Half of the firms – the least productive ones – see a decline in their productivity following tighter environmental policy. This significant negative effect at the firm level is compatible with the industry-level results because the firm-level analysis focuses on surviving firms while the industry-level analysis also accounts for entry and exit. Environmental policies may force the least-productive firms to exit the market and trigger a reallocation of factors towards more productive or new firms. The analysis also finds heterogeneous effects depending on the design of environmental policy, in line with the narrow version of the Porter Hypothesis. Market-based environmental policies are found to be more productivity-friendly than non-market-based ones.

Limitations: Evidence is limited to OECD countries; the channels at work are not analysed

While this analysis provides one of the first large-scale studies of the Porter Hypothesis, it is still limited to OECD countries only. Extending the stringency measure would allow to include developing countries and emerging economies into the analysis. While the EPS indicator provides the most comprehensive indicator of environmental policies related to air and climate, it is not without limitations; for example, it does not account for enforcement (Chapter 1). This study is also only able to provide insights into overall effects on productivity, without being able to detect the actual channels at work behind these effects. Whether productivity increases through changes in investment patterns, entry and exit, international trade, relocation, or employment is not covered in this study (see Chapters 3 to 9 for in-depth studies of these channels).

A stronger focus on market-based policies is needed

Market-based environmental policy instruments are found to be more friendly to productivity growth than non-market instruments. Explicit price signals provide firms with higher flexibility in the abatement process, by allowing them to choose either the most suitable technology solution or the timing of the adjustment. These findings can be seen as tentative support for the idea that market-based instruments are more cost-effective than command-and-control policies, including through their effects on productivity.

Notes

[1] This chapter is a summary of the paper Albrizio, Koźluk and Zipperer (2017[24]), "Environmental policies and productivity growth: Evidence across industries and firms", Journal of Environmental Economics and Management, 81, 209-226, which originated from the OECD Working Paper "Empirical Evidence on the Effects of Environmental Policy Stringency on Productivity Growth" by Albrizio, Koźluk and Zipperer (2014[27]), OECD Economics Department Working Papers, No. 1179. Preceding work also includes the OECD Working Paper "Environmental Policies and Productivity Growth: A Critical Review of Empirical Findings" by Koźluk and Zipperer (2014[5]), OECD Economics Department Working Papers, No. 1096.

[2] The OECD's Productivity by industry (PDBi) database has been discontinued. Annual sectoral statistics on productivity growth are now available within the "Productivity and ULC by Main Economic Activity" database (https://stats.oecd.org/Index.aspx?DataSetCode=PDBI_I4).

[3] Specifically this excludes countries that have a fossil fuel electricity generation capacity share below 30%, which excludes Norway, France, Sweden and Canada in their analysis.

References

Acemoglu, D., P. Aghion and F. Zilibotti (2006), "Distance to Frontier, Selection and Economic Growth", *Journal of the European Economic Association*, Vol. 4/1, pp. 37-74, https://economics.mit.edu/files/4472. [19]

Aghion, P. and P. Howitt (2006), "Joseph Schumpeter Lecture: Appropriate Policy Growth: A Unifying Framework", *Journal of the European Economic Association*, Vol. 4/2-3, pp. 269-314. [20]

Albrizio, S., T. Koźluk and V. Zipperer (2017), "Environmental policies and productivity growth: Evidence across industries and firms", *Journal of Environmental Econonics and Management*, Vol. 81, pp. 209-226. [24]

Albrizio, S., T. Koźluk and V. Zipperer (2014), "Empirical evidence on the effects of environmental policy stringency on productivity growth", *OECD Economics Department Working Papers*, Vol. 1179, https://doi.org/10.1787/5jxrjnb36b40-en. [27]

Alpay, E., S. Buccola and J. Kerkvliet (2002), "Productivity Growth and Environmental Regulation in Mexican and U.S. Food Manufacturing", *American Journal of Agricultural Economics*, Vol. 84/4, pp. 887-901, https://doi.org/10.1111/1467-8276.00041. [15]

Ambec, S. et al. (2013), "The porter hypothesis at 20 Can environmental regulation enhance innovation and competitiveness?", *Review of Environmental Economics and Policy*, Vol. 7/1, pp. 2-22. [6]

Barbera, A. and V. McConnell (1990), "The Impact of Environmental Regulations on Industry Productivity: Direct and Indirect Effects", *Journal of Environmental Economics and Management*, Vol. 18/1, pp. 50-65, https://doi.org/10.1016/0095-0696(90)90051-Y. [8]

Becker, R. (2011), "Local environmental regulation and plant-level productivity", *Ecological Economics*, Vol. 70/12, pp. 2513-2522, https://doi.org/10.1016/j.ecolecon.2011.08.019. [16]

Botta, E. and T. Koźluk (2014), "Measuring environmental policy stringency in OECD countries", *Economics Department Working Papers*, No. 1177, OECD, Paris, https://doi.org/10.1787/5jxrjnc45gvg-en (accessed on 17 January 2019). [18]

Bourlès, R. et al. (2013), "Do Product Market Regulations In Upstream Sectors Curb Productivity Growth? Panel Data Evidence For OECD Countries", *Review of Economics and Statistics*, Vol. 95/5, pp. 1750-1768, http://dx.doi.org/10.1162/REST_a_00338. [22]

Cohen, M. and A. Tubb (2017), "The impact of Environmental Regulation on Firm and Country Competitiveness: A Meta-Analysis of the Porter Hypothesis", *Journal of the Association of Environmental and Resource Economists*, Vol. 5/2, https://doi.org/10.1086/695613. [4]

Dufour, C., P. Lanoie and M. Patry (1998), "Regulation and productivity", *Journal of Productivity Analysis*, Vol. 9/3, pp. 233-247, https://link.springer.com/article/10.1023/A:1018387021327. [9]

Franco, C. and G. Marin (2017), "The effect of within-sector, upstream and downstream environmental taxes on innovation and productivity", *Environment and Resource Economics*, pp. 261-291. [13]

Gal, P. (2013), "Measuring Total Factor Productivity at the Firm level using OECD-ORBIS", *OECD Economics Department Working Papers no. 1049*, https://www.oecd-ilibrary.org/economics/measuring-total-factor-productivity-at-the-firm-level-using-oecd-orbis_5k46dsb25ls6-en. [26]

Gray, W. (1987), "The Cost of Regulation: OSHA, EPA and the Productivity Slowdown", *The American Economic Review*, Vol. 77/5, pp. 998-1006, https://www.jstor.org/stable/1810223?seq=1#metadata_info_tab_contents. [7]

Gray, W. and R. Shadbegian (2003), "Plant vintage, technology, and environmental regulation", *Journal of Environmental Economics and Management*, Vol. 46/3, pp. 384-402, https://doi.org/10.1016/S0095-0696(03)00031-7. [17]

Hamamoto, M. (2006), "Environmental regulation and the productivity of Japanese manufacturing industries", *Resource and energy economics*, Vol. 28/4, pp. 299-312, https://doi.org/10.1016/j.reseneeco.2005.11.001. [10]

Jaffe, A. and K. Palmer (1997), "Environmental regulation and innovation: a panel data study", *The Review of Economics and Statistics*, Vol. 79/4, pp. 610-619. [3]

Koźluk, T. and V. Zipperer (2014), "Environmental policies and productivity growth: a critical review of empirical findings", *OECD Journal: Economic Studies*, Vol. 2014/1, https://dx.doi.org/10.1787/eco_studies-2014-5jz2drqml75j. [5]

Lanoie, P., M. Patry and J. Lajeunesse (2008), "Environmental Regulation and Productivity: New Findings on the Porter Hypothesis", *Journal of Productivity Analysis* 30, pp. 121-128. [12]

Nicoletti, G. and S. Scarpetta (2003), "Regulation, Productivity and Growth: OECD Evidence", *OECD Economics Department Working Papers*, No. 347, OECD Publishing, Paris, https://dx.doi.org/10.1787/078677503357. [21]

Porter, M. (1991), "America's green strategy", *Scientific American*, Vol. 264/4, p. 168. [2]

Porter, M. and C. van der Linde (1995), "Toward a New Conception of the Environment-Competitiveness Relationship", *Journal of Economic Perspectives*, Vol. 9/4, pp. 97-118, http://dx.doi.org/10.1257/jep.9.4.97. [1]

Rajan, R. and L. Zingales (1998), "Financial Dependence and Growth", *The American Economic Review*, Vol. 88/3, pp. 559-586, https://www.jstor.org/stable/116849?seq=1#metadata_info_tab_contents. [23]

Rubashkina, Y., M. Galeotti and E. Verdolini (2015), "Environmental regulation and competitiveness: empirical evidence on the Porter Hypothesis from European manufacturing sectors", *Energy Policy*, Vol. 83, pp. 288-300. [14]

Wooldridge, J. (2009), "On estimating firm-level productivity functions using proxy variables to control for unobservables", *Economics Letters*, Vol. 104. [25]

Yang, C., Y. Tseng and C. Chen (2012), "Environmental regulations, induced R&D, and productivity: Evidence from Taiwan's manufacturing industries", *Resource and Energy Economics*, Vol. 34/4, pp. 514-532, https://doi.org/10.1016/j.reseneeco.2012.05.001. [11]

3 Firm employment, energy prices and environmental policy stringency

Employment effects of tighter environmental policies are the focus of this chapter.[1] By increasing production costs, unilateral environmental policies might hamper the competitiveness of industries, leading to output contraction and job losses. The potential impacts on employment are probably the main concern for policy makers when implementing stricter environmental policies, but the empirical evidence on this effect is limited so far. This study provides an empirical evaluation of the impact of increased energy prices and more stringent environmental policies as measured by the OECD Environmental Policy Stringency (EPS) Indicator on employment. It uses a combination of firm- and sector-level datasets across OECD countries over the period 2000-14. The results at the sectoral level show a significant negative effect on average of changes in energy prices as well as of changes in the environmental policy stringency index. The magnitude of the effect is, however, small: a 10% increase in energy prices leads to a reduction of 0.7% in manufacturing employment. Energy-intensive sectors see a stronger decline in employment due to higher energy prices, but less energy-intensive sectors do not show any significant effect. The firm-level analysis shows that higher energy prices have a small positive effect on the employment level of surviving firms while increasing the probability of firm exit. Tighter environmental policies on the other hand show a small negative effect on the employment level of surviving firms while not affecting firm entry or exit.

Background

A strong negative correlation between energy prices and employment

Political debates often use the potential negative effects on employment as an argument against the introduction of tighter environmental policies. Additional compliance costs are assumed to increase production costs, thereby lowering the international competitiveness of the industry, leading to an output contraction and consequent lay-offs. Energy-intensive sectors are expected to be particularly affected. Figure 3.1. shows the evolution of employment in the manufacturing sector together with average energy prices across OECD countries between 2000 and 2014. A strong negative correlation can be observed, which – despite having no causal interpretation – helps explain why the debate around new or stricter environmental regulations is often framed in terms of "jobs versus the environment" (Morgenstern, Pizer and Shih, 2002[1]).

Theory predicts no long-run effects but potential short-term adjustments

Theoretically, in the long-run, there should be no sustained effects of tighter environmental policies on employment. Sectors losing out in terms of competitiveness might shed labour, but in the long term, an adjustment in the labour market should take place, shifting employment towards less polluting sectors, leaving total unemployment unchanged (Fankhauser, Sehhleier and Stern, 2008[2]). In the short term, there might, however, be adjustment costs through two effects: a demand effect (employment losses due to a contraction of output) and a substitution effect (a shift from capital towards labour in the production process due to an increase in the effective rental rate of productive capital). Whether the overall short-run employment effect is positive or negative depends in particular on the relative labour-intensity of polluting and non-polluting activities (Morgenstern, Pizer and Shih, 2002[1]; Dechenes, 2011[3]).

Figure 3.1. Employment and energy price trends over time for OECD countries

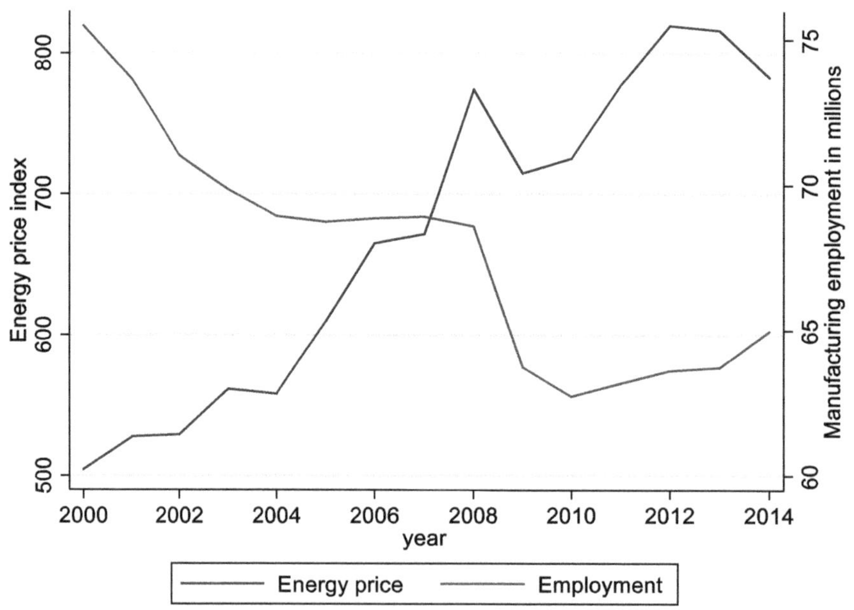

Note: The Figure shows average trends in energy prices and employment for OECD countries.
Source: Dechezleprêtre, Nachtigall and Stadler (2020[4]).

Empirical studies suggest a small negative effect on employment

Empirical studies that have evaluated the effects of more stringent environmental policies suggest that there is either no or a small negative employment effect in the short run, mostly in energy-intensive sectors (see Dechezleprêtre, Nachtigall and Stadler (2020[4]) for a detailed review of the literature). The approaches taken in the studies vary from investigating the United States Clean Air Act (Greenstone, 2002[5]; Kahn, 1997[6]; Walker, 2013[7]), using pollution abatement costs as a measure for environmental policy stringency (Morgenstern, Pizer and Shih, 2002[1]; Belova et al., 2013[8]), to comparing regulated to non-regulated plants (Berman and Bui, 2001[9]; Cole and Elliott, 2007[10]; Ferris, Shadbegian and Wolverton, 2014[11]). More recent studies have specifically looked at the effect of energy prices on employment (Dechenes, 2011[3]; Kahn and Mansur, 2013[12]; Hille and Möbius, 2019[13]), finding insignificant or weakly negative effects for the average industry and a negative effect for energy-intensive sectors. Studies looking specifically at employment effects of the European Union Emissions Trading Scheme find no statistically significant effects (see Dechezleprêtre, Nachtigall and Venmans (2018[14]) (summarised in Chapter 7); others include Martin et al. (2014[15]); Anger and Oberndorfer (Anger and Oberndorfer, 2008[16]); Commins et al. (2011[17]); Abrell, Ndoye Faye and Zachmann (2011[18]); Chan, Li and Zhang (2013[19]). Country-specific studies find reallocation effects in the labour market due to higher energy prices, implying that larger, energy-inefficient firms reduce their number of employees, while employment rises in energy-efficient firms, leaving overall employment at the industry level largely unaffected (see Dussaux (2020[20]) and Dechezleprêtre and Brucal (2021[21]), summarised in Chapter 8 and 9).

Contribution of this study – a large-scale dataset allowing for heterogeneous effects, investigating energy prices and environmental policies

This study offers three main contributions to the literature. First, it reassesses the existing evidence of environmental policies on manufacturing sector-level employment using both energy prices as well as the OECD's EPS indicator as measures of environmental policy stringency (see Box 1.3 in Chapter 1 for a discussion of different measures of environmental regulation). This analysis is based on data from the World Input Output Database, covering OECD countries over the period 2000 to 2014.[2] Second, the sector-level analysis is complemented by firm-level evidence based on a large-scale dataset, covering more than 500 000 firms located in 23 countries. The large dataset allows to identify heterogeneous effects among countries, sectors and firm types. The main limitation of firm-level data is that only surviving firms are observed. Third, to address this shortcoming, the analysis also looks at firm entry and exit, using the OECD-Eurostat Business Demography Statistics.

Empirical set-up

Assessing the effects of energy prices and other environmental policies

Climate change policies such as carbon taxes or carbon markets would primarily affect firms through raising energy prices. Therefore, energy prices are informative about the likely effect of future market-based policy interventions to reduce carbon emissions. However, price-based mechanisms which translate into higher energy prices are only one type of environmental policy. There also exist numerous other instruments such as emission standards or taxes on pollutants other than CO_2 (e.g. NO_x, SO_x) which are all reflected in the OECD's environmental policy stringency indicator (EPS). Therefore, both energy prices and the OECD EPS are used to investigate the employment effects of environmental policies. Interestingly, the correlation between within-country year-on-year changes in energy prices and in the EPS is very low (<0.1), so that both variables provide independent sources of variation which can be exploited in the empirical analysis.

Empirical model

The empirical model used here relies on a specification that is commonly used by most studies on this topic (e.g. Hille and Möbius (2019[13])) and is estimated for the industry- and firm-level. The following equation is estimated:

$$\ln(y_{cst}) = \beta_p \ln(p_{cst-1}) + \beta_s \ln(s_{ct-1}) + \beta_w \ln(w_{cst-1}) + \beta_x X_{cst-1} + \alpha_{cs} + \delta_t + \mu_{ct} + \chi_{st} + \varepsilon_{cst}$$

where $\ln(y_{cst})$ is the log employment of sector s (or firm i) in country c and in year t. p_{cst} indicates the energy price in sector s and country c in year *t*, and is measured as sector-specific consumption shares of different fuel types, using time-fixed weights for aggregation in order to filter out the changes in energy prices related to changes in fuel prices or energy taxes instead of capturing changes in fuel choices (Sato et al., 2019[22]). s_{ct-1} is the OECD environmental policy stringency indicator (which, for the firm-level analysis, is interacted with the sectoral energy-intensity). w_{cst-1} is the average hourly real wage in sector *s* and country *c*. The energy prices as well as the wage variable are lagged by one year to reduce problems of reverse causality and to account for potential time lags in the effect of energy prices on employment. The vector X_{cst-1} represents further control variables, namely the log of capital and the log of value added per worker (at the sector or firm level). α_{cs} represents sector (or firm) fixed effects, depending on the specification, to control for time-invariant differences across sectors or firms, which might be correlated with both employment and energy prices. δ_t represent year fixed effects, capturing global shocks common to all countries and sectors, such as changes in global crude oil prices. In the sector-level analysis, μ_{ct} captures quadratic trends at the country level, χ_{st} captures quadratic trends at the sector level. In the firm-level analysis, μ_{ct} and χ_{st} are country-by-year and sector-by-year fixed effects.[3] ε_{cst} represents the remaining error term.

Data

The final sample of the sector-level analysis covers 28 OECD countries and 19 different manufacturing sectors from 2000 to 2014. The sector-level wage data are sourced from the World Input Output Database (WIOD). The final sample of the firm-level analysis covers half a million firms, operating in 340 different sub-sectors, being located in 23 OECD economies, and spans the time period from 2000 to 2014. The firm-level employment data are drawn from the OECD version of the ORBIS database from the Bureau Van Dijk. The analysis uses energy prices from Sato et al. (2019), and the OECD EPS indicator (Botta and Koźluk, 2014[23]). As EPS varies at the country-year level, it is interacted with the sector-specific energy-intensity in the firm-level analysis, following the approach of Rajan and Zingales (1998[24]).

Results

Negative but small decline in employment in response to higher energy prices and tighter environmental policies

The empirical analysis uses changes in country- and sector-specific energy prices to estimate the effect on employment. The results of the main specification at the sector-level show a significant negative effect of changes in country-sector specific energy prices and of increasing sector-specific environmental policy stringency on employment (Table 3.1). However, the effects are small: a 10% increase in energy prices, which is experienced every four to five years in the typical country in the sample, would reduce employment by 0.7 per cent. Similarly, a 10% increase in the EPS indicator would lead to a reduction of employment by 0.58 per cent. The firm-level estimation shows a different picture: Increasing energy prices are on average found to be significantly positively related with firm employment while tighter environmental policy stringency measures by the EPS index is found to be significantly negatively related. Again, the effects are small: A 10% increase in energy prices would increase employment by 0.66%, a 10% increase in EPS would reduce employment by 0.4%.

Table 3.1. Employment effects - main estimation results

	Sector-level			Firm-level		
Dep. variable: log of employment	(1)	(2)	(3)	(1)	(2)	(3)
Log energy price (t – 1)	-0.070***	-0.054*		0.066***	0.057***	
	(-0.032)	(0.029)		(0.016)	(0.016)	
Log EPS (t - 1)	-0.058***		-0.049***	-0.040***		-0.031**
	(0.015)		(0.014)	(0.015)		(0.015)
Log hourly wage (t - 1)	-0.115***	-0.107***	-0.113***	-0.058***	-0.057***	-0.060***
	(0.041)	(0.042)	(0.040)	(0.008)	(0.008)	(0.008)
Log capital (t - 1)	0.187***	0.187***	0.185***	0.119***	0.119***	0.119***
	(0.042)	(0.042)	(0.041)	(0.001)	(0.001)	(0.001)
Log value added per worker (t - 1)	-0.014	-0.022	-0.013	-0.034***	-0.034***	-0.034***
	(0.039)	(0.038)	(0.039)	(0.001)	(0.001)	(0.001)
Number of observations	6494	7502	6566	2510413	2510413	2510413

Notes: Standard errors are shown in parentheses and are clustered at the firm or sector level, depending on the specification. Significance levels are given by: * p<0.1, ** p<0.05 and *** p<0.01.

Energy-intensive sectors face a larger negative effect on employment than other sectors

Interacting the energy price and the EPS variable with sector-specific dummy variables allows to estimate heterogeneous sectoral effects. Based on the sector-level results, these estimations show that the negative effect on employment is larger for more energy-intensive sectors, as shown in Figure 3.2. (Panel A). The iron and steel sector, transport equipment and petrochemicals are the most affected sectors when energy prices rise. Changes in the EPS mostly affect employment in the transport equipment sector, machinery and petrochemicals sector (Panel B in Figure 3.2.).

Figure 3.2. Sector heterogeneous effects on employment

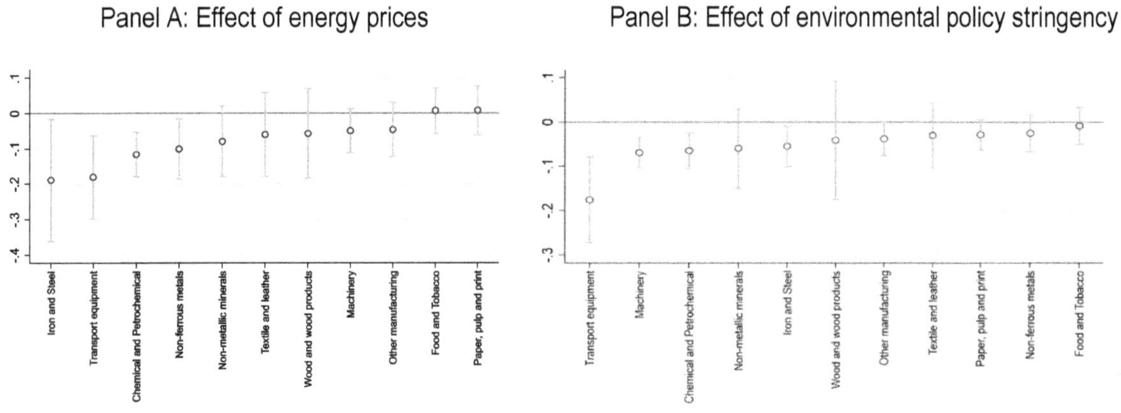

Note: The figure shows the point estimates and 95% confidence intervals of the energy price variable and the EPS variable respectively on the log of employment.

Difference in industry- and firm-level results are driven by a positive effect on the exit of firms

A further analysis uses information on the entry and exit of firms and reveals that the difference in industry- and firm-level results comes from a positive effect of energy prices on firm exit. Higher energy prices increase the exit of firms. As higher energy prices trigger firms to exit the market, surviving firms are able to grow and increase the number of employees. There is evidence found in the analysis that surviving firms indeed expand in response to increasing energy prices through an increase in gross output. The aggregate effect on employment remains negative, however, explaining the divergent results found at the sector- and firm-level. Changes in the EPS do not have an effect on firm exit nor on gross output. The negative effect found at the firm level of increasing EPS seems to be the major driver for the negative results found at the sector-level.

Robustness checks of firm level analysis

The results are robust to several robustness checks. Different lag structures are tested, a first-difference specification is employed as an alternative way to account for firm-specific heterogeneity, and a range of further sector-level controls were introduced. None of these robustness checks show significantly different results.

Conclusion

A small employment effect on average – but stronger in energy-intensive sectors

The results of this study show that there is a small statistically significant negative effect of changes in energy prices as well as changes of environmental policy stringency on sector-level employment on average. At the firm-level, there is a slight statistically significant positive effect on firm-level employment of increasing energy prices, while the effect of a tightening of environmental policies remains negative at the firm-level. The different results at the firm- and sector-level for energy prices are explained by a rising level of firm exits due to rising energy prices. The effects are heterogeneous across sectors, with the most energy-intensive sectors facing the largest decline in employment. The magnitude of the effect in energy-intensive sectors is, however, small: in the iron and steel sector, a 10% increase in the price of energy reduces firm employment by 0.2%. For the United States, this number would translate into slightly more than 1 000 lost jobs per year, accounting for around 7% of total employment losses in the US steel sector.

An upper bound of the true effect?

The analysis has two main limitations. First, to the extent that changes in energy prices or environmental regulations induce a rapid shift in demand (and thus employment) from strict to less-strictly regulated sectors and regions, estimates of employment losses presented here would be biased upward. The extent of such general equilibrium effects are difficult to estimate, but the results should be understood as an upper-bound of the true effect of higher energy prices and stricter environmental policies. Second, the results are only valid in the short run. In the longer run, there might be no net effect on job losses as workers move from contracting or exiting firms to other firms or other sectors (in particular, the analysis focuses on the manufacturing sector, but affected workers might find jobs in the services sector).

Complementary policies to ease transition costs

The analysis clearly demonstrates that there exist transition costs in the short run, when stricter environmental policies are imposed, as some workers are forced to move away from affected firms and sectors, even if many of these job losses are unlikely to be permanent as laid-off workers may ultimately find other jobs. Because these reallocation effects have redistributive implications and generate costs for laid-off workers, these results call for complementary labour market policies that minimise those costs on affected workers and ease between-firm adjustments in employment. Moreover, since these transition costs are typically highly localised in regions specialised in polluting activities, they can also translate into potentially significant regional effects and thus political costs.

Effects on types of workers and on wages remain outside of the scope of this study

The analysis could be complemented with an assessment of the effect of energy prices and EPS across different types of workers (high-skilled versus low-skilled) and across types of regions (e.g. rural versus urban). Another complementary analysis could focus on employees' wages rather than on the number of employees. Additional data on employees and on firm location would allow for such analyses.

Notes

[1] This chapter is a summary of the paper "The effect of energy prices and environmental policy stringency on manufacturing employment in OECD countries: Sector- and firm-level evidence" by A. Dechezleprêtre, D. Nachtigall and B. Stadler, *OECD Economics Department Working Papers* (2020), OECD Publishing, Paris.

[2] Energy price levels between 2000 and 2014 may not be entirely representative of energy price developments in more recent years. The empirical analysis does however not analyse the effect of energy price *levels*, but uses within-firm or within-sector *changes* in energy prices to identify the effect. To derive implications for future changes in energy prices, one needs to assume that past changes in energy prices and their effect on employment are representative of future changes in energy prices and their effect on employment. If energy prices change drastically in the future, the effects on employment may differ from the effects estimated based on past changes in energy prices.

[3] As EPS varies at the country-year level, it is interacted with the sector-specific energy-intensity in the firm-level analysis, following the approach of Rajan and Zingales (1998[24]).

References

Abrell, J., A. Ndoye Faye and G. Zachmann (2011), "Assessing the impact of the EU ETS using firm level data", *Bruegel Working Paper*, https://www.bruegel.org/2011/07/assessing-the-impact-of-the-eu-ets-using-firm-level-data/. [18]

Anger, N. and U. Oberndorfer (2008), "Firm performance and employment in the EU emissions trading scheme: An empirical assessment for Germany", *Energy Policy*, Vol. 36/1, pp. 12-22, https://doi.org/10.1016/j.enpol.2007.09.007. [16]

Belova, A. et al. (2013), "Environmental Regulation and Industry Employment: A Reassessment", *US Census Bureau Center for Economic Studies Paper*, Vol. CES-WP-13-36, https://www2.census.gov/ces/wp/2013/CES-WP-13-36.pdf. [8]

Berman, E. and L. Bui (2001), "Environmental regulation and productivity: evidence from oil refineries", *Review of Economics and Statistics*, Vol. 83/3, pp. 498-510, https://www.mitpressjournals.org/doi/pdf/10.1162/003465301524801 44. [9]

Botta, E. and T. Koźluk (2014), "Measuring environmental policy stringency in OECD countries", *Economics Department Working Papers*, No. 1177, OECD, Paris, https://doi.org/10.1787/5jxrjnc45gvg-en (accessed on 17 January 2019). [23]

Brucal, A. and A. Dechezleprêtre (2021), "Assessing the impact of energy prices on plant-level environmental and economic performance: Evidence from Indonesian manufacturers", *OECD Environment Working Papers, No. 170*, https://doi.org/10.1787/9ec54222-en. [21]

Chan, H., S. Li and F. Zhang (2013), "Firm competitiveness and the European Union emissions trading scheme", *Energy Policy*, Vol. 63, pp. 1056-1064, https://doi.org/10.1016/j.enpol.2013.09.032. [19]

Cole, M. and R. Elliott (2007), "Do environmental regulations cost jobs? An industry-level analysis of the UK", *The BE Journal of Economic Analysis & Policy*, Vol. 7/1, https://doi.org/10.2202/1935-1682.1668. [10]

Commins, N. et al. (2011), "Climate Policy & Corporate Behavior", *Energy Journal*, Vol. 32/4, pp. 51-68, https://www.jstor.org/stable/41323333. [17]

Dechenes, O. (2011), "Climate policy and labor markets", in Fullerton, D. and C. Wolfram (eds.), *The design and implementation of US climate policy*, University of Chicago Press, Chicago, http://www.nber.org/chapters/c12150.pdf (accessed on 25 January 2019). [3]

Dechezleprêtre, A., D. Nachtigall and B. Stadler (2020), "The effect of energy prices and environmental policy stringency on manufacturing employment in OECD countries: Sector- and firm-level evidence", *OECD Economics Department Working Papers*, No. 1625, OECD Publishing, Paris, https://dx.doi.org/10.1787/899eb13f-en. [4]

Dechezleprêtre, A., D. Nachtigall and F. Venmans (2018), "The joint impact of the European Union emissions trading system on carbon emissions and economic performance", *OECD Economics Department Working Papers*, No. 1515, OECD Publishing, Paris, https://dx.doi.org/10.1787/4819b016-en. [14]

Dussaux, D. (2020), "The joint effects of energy prices and carbon taxes on environmental and economic performance: Evidence from the French manufacturing sector", *OECD Environment Working Papers*, No. 154, OECD Publishing, Paris, https://dx.doi.org/10.1787/b84b1b7d-en. [20]

Fankhauser, S., F. Sehhleier and N. Stern (2008), "Climate change, innovation and jobs", *Climate Policy*, Vol. 8/4, pp. 421-429, http://dx.doi.org/doi:10.3763/cpol.2008.0513. [2]

Ferris, A., R. Shadbegian and A. Wolverton (2014), "The Effect of Environmental Regulation on Power Sector Employment: Phase I of the Title IV SO2 Trading Program", *Journal of the Association of Environmental and Resource Economists*, Vol. 1/4, pp. 521-553, http://dx.doi.org/10.1086/679301. [11]

Greenstone, M. (2002), "The Impacts of Environmental Regulations on Industrial Activity: Evidence from the 1970 and 1977 Clean Air Act Amendments and the Census of Manufacturers", *Journal of Political Economy*, pp. 1175-1219, https://www.jstor.org/stable/10.1086/342808. [5]

Hille, E. and P. Möbius (2019), “Do energy prices affect employment? Decomposed international evidence”, *Journal of Environmental Economics and Management*, Vol. 96, pp. 1-21, https://doi.org/10.1016/j.jeem.2019.04.002. [13]

Kahn, M. (1997), “Particulate pollution trends in the United States”, *Regional Science and Urban Economics*, Vol. 27/1, pp. 87-107, https://doi.org/10.1016/S0166-0462(96)02144-8. [6]

Kahn, M. and E. Mansur (2013), “Do local energy prices and regulation affect the geographic concentration of employment?”, *Journal of Public Economics*, Vol. 101, pp. 105-114, https://doi.org/10.1016/j.jpubeco.2013.03.002. [12]

Martin, R. et al. (2014), “Industry Compensation under Relocation Risk: A firm-level analysis of the EU Emissions Trading Scheme”, *The American Economic Review*, Vol. 104/8, pp. 2482-2508, https://www.aeaweb.org/articles?id=10.1257/aer.104.8.2482. [15]

Morgenstern, R., W. Pizer and J. Shih (2002), “Jobs versus the environment: An industry-level perspective”, *Journal of Environmental Economics and Management*, Vol. 43/3, pp. 412-436, https://doi.org/10.1006/jeem.2001.1191. [1]

Rajan, R. and L. Zingales (1998), “Financial Dependence and Growth”, *The American Economic Review*, Vol. 88/3, pp. 559-586, https://www.jstor.org/stable/116849?seq=1#metadata_info_tab_contents. [24]

Sato, M. et al. (2019), “International and sectoral variation in industry energy prices 1995-2015”, *Energy Economics*, Vol. 78, pp. 235-258. [22]

Walker, W. (2013), “The transitional costs of sectoral reallocation: evidence from the Clean Air Act and the workforce”, *The Quarterly Journal of Economics*, Vol. 1787, https://doi.org/10.1093/qje/qjt022. [7]

4 Induced investment through environmental policies

Investment decisions of firms are the focus of this chapter.[1] Adapting to new environmental regulations ultimately requires investment by firms. These could be investment in abatement capital or more environmentally-friendly/less polluting machines. Firms could respond by downsizing their capital investment or increasing investment and thereby modernising their capital stock. They might also shift more of their capital investment into foreign countries, circumventing stricter environmental regulations at home. The empirical literature on the investment responses of firms to stricter environmental policies has been inconclusive so far. This study sheds more light into this relationship by estimating a reduced-form model of firms' capital demand. Using sector-specific energy prices as a proxy for environmental policies, this study analyses data on over 12 000 listed firms in 30 OECD countries over the period 1995 to 2011 and is able to differentiate investment effects across sectors as well as across domestic and foreign capital investment, contributing to the empirical evidence around the so-called Pollution Haven Hypothesis. The results show that higher energy prices are associated with a small but significant decrease in total investment, though in the most energy-intensive sectors, total investment increases. Differentiating between domestic and foreign investment shows that domestic investment of all sectors is negatively correlated with increasing energy prices, indicating that energy-intensive sectors offshore some of their investment to foreign countries.

Background

Environmental policies need to incentivise investment in carbon-saving production processes

Limiting global warming to below 2°C requires significant investment into new technologies and low-carbon production processes in the manufacturing industries. Around one fifth of total greenhouse gas emissions globally are directly emitted by the industrial sector (IPCC, 2014[1]). This makes it one of the key players to reduce emissions in order to achieve the goals formulated in the Paris Agreement signed at the UN Climate Change Conference in 2015. The path to limiting global warming to (less than) 2°C implies a reduction of emissions in the manufacturing sector by 19% to 38%, depending on industry classifications and methodology (McKinsey, 2013[2]; OECD, 2012[3]). These reductions can only be achieved with substantial investment into more efficient production processes – be it in terms of energy, CO_2 or material efficiency.[2]

Environmental policies may reduce investment through output reductions

In order to design policies that incentivise low-carbon investment, policy makers need to better understand the implications of environmental policies on investment undertaken by firms. While the objective of environmental policies is to contribute to better environmental outcomes, these policies will likely affect production costs of firms and thus investment. This effect could work through the acquisition of abatement capital such as end-of-pipe technologies or through a more complex re-design of production processes towards low-carbon production, e.g. requiring new machinery investment.

The net effect on investment is unclear a priori

Whether total investment increases or decreases in response to environmental policies is unclear a priori. The theoretical literature suggests that the total effect on investment depends on the size of the downsizing and the modernisation effect (Xepapadeas and de Zeeuw, 1998[4]). On the one hand, a tightening of environmental policies might increase input costs (e.g. of energy), which lead to increased production costs and decreased output via a downsizing effect – which will eventually also affect investment. On the other hand, increased input costs such as rising energy prices might have a modernisation effect, incentivising firms to switch from old energy-intensive to new, more energy-efficient machines. Whether the reduced investment from the downsizing effect outweighs the increased investment into new capital through the modernisation effect is, however, not clear a priori.

Investment effects depend on the substitutability of inputs

The direction of the effect of increased input costs through environmental policies on total investment also depends on the substitutability between the various production inputs. Particularly energy as a production input might become more expensive in response to tighter environmental policies. If energy and capital are complements as inputs, then higher energy prices will likely lead to a reduction of energy input use and thus require less capital. If energy input and capital input are substitutes, then higher energy prices might lead to a reduction in the use of energy as an input and to an increase of capital at the same time (Constantini and Paglialunga, 2014[5]). Determining this elasticity of substitution, however, difficult as it is, depends on the modelling assumptions of production functions.

The effects on domestic and foreign investment are potentially heterogeneous

It is important to disentangle the effect of higher energy prices on domestic versus foreign investment. According to the Pollution Haven Hypothesis, tighter environmental policy might lead firms to shift their production to less stringent countries, thereby keeping production costs low but potentially keeping emissions at the same level globally. This effect might increase the foreign direct investment of firms, leading to higher investment of firms. It might, however, also come at the expense of domestic investment which could be reduced, leading to lower investment. An increase in investment might thus not imply a positive environmental outcome as emissions might just have been shifted to another country.

The literature is inconclusive so far

The empirical evidence on investment effects of environmental policies is limited and inconclusive so far (see Dlugosch and Koźluk (2017[6]) for more detail). Country-specific analyses of the United States tend to associate tighter environmental policies with a downsizing effect and thus lower investment (Greenstone, 2002[7]; Nelson, Tietenburg and Donihue, 1993[8]) while a study on Japan found support for a stronger modernisation effect (Hamamoto, 2006[9]). The only cross-country study so far focuses on European economies and finds evidence for a stronger modernisation effect for machinery, buildings and total investment (Leiter, Parolini and Winner, 2011[10]). Differentiating between investment into productive capital and pollution abatement capital (e.g. filters and scrubbers), early empirical evidence from the United States hints at a crowding-out effect of investment in pollution abatement on productive investment (Garofalo and Malhotra, 1995[11]; Gray and Shadbegian, 1998[12]) whereas more recent empirical evidence from the United Kingdom finds that total investment is unaffected, while investment into environmentally friendly technologies increased (Kneller and Manerson, 2012[13]).

This study: the first large-scale panel analysis with heterogeneous effects across sectors

This study provides the first large-scale cross-country study on the investment effects of increased environmental protection efforts. Using sector-specific energy prices as a proxy for environmental policies, this study analyses data on 12 619 listed firms in 30 OECD countries over the period 1995 to 2011, estimating a reduced-form model of firms' capital demand. While the sample only contains listed firms, the behaviour of this set of firms helps explain a major part of aggregate fluctuations (Gabaix, 2011[14]). By using sector-specific energy prices and firm-level capital investment data, this study is able to differentiate investment effects across sectors, with a special focus on clean versus dirty sectors. Furthermore, by differentiating between domestic and foreign capital investment, this study is able to investigate whether firms offshore some of their production to other countries in response to increasing energy prices, contributing empirical evidence for or against the so-called Pollution Haven hypothesis.

Empirical set-up

Capital demand derived from a three-factor production function

The empirical analysis is based on a model of the firm's optimal capital demand. A three-factor production function, where the inputs are capital, labour and energy, is used as the basis to model the firm's capital demand. As the demand for capital depends on the inputs and their respective prices (Holly and Smith, 1989[15]), a change in input prices due to changes in the business environment thus implies changes in the capital stock. These changes depend on the substitutability between inputs. The changes in energy prices could thus translate directly into changes in the capital stock.

Empirical model

Firm-level investment is measured as the ratio of capital expenditure over the capital stock. The following equation is then estimated:

$$I_{isct} = +\beta_1 \Delta EPI_{sct-1} + \sum_j \gamma_j X_{isct}^j + \sum_t \theta_t d_t + \alpha_i + \varepsilon_{isct}$$

where I_{isct} is investment defined as $I_{isct} = \frac{CE_{isct}}{K_{isct}}$, with CE_{isct} being the capital expenditure and K_{isct} the capital stock. ΔEPI_{sct-1} measures the three-year moving average of energy price changes, X_{isct} is a vector of control variables, d are year dummies, α are firm fixed effects, and ε is the error term. The indices *i* indicate firms, *s* sectors, *c* countries and *t* time. Similar to the analysis of productivity effects in Chapter 2, a three-year moving average of the energy price is used here as it is assumed that investment takes time (decision making process, implementation etc.). The control variables X include the current level of firm sales scaled by total assets as a demand proxy, as well as country-specific variables like the output gap, real interest rates, an employment protection legislation indicator (EPL), an indicator for financial development and a regulatory impact indicator (see Dlugosch and Koźluk (2017[6]) for more detail). The EPL and the financial development variables are interacted with sector-level variables (lay-off rates and dependency on external finance, respectively) in order to allow for sector-level heterogeneity of these variables.

Identification of the effect

The effect of increasing energy prices is identified through the within-firm time-series variation of investment. The firm fixed effects control for firm-specific time-invariant characteristics that might influence investment decisions and might be correlated with energy prices (such as management performance or human capital endowment effects, which might be associated with higher investment and lower energy prices). The time dummies control for global shocks, e.g. supply shocks or energy price shocks, which are correlated with both investment and energy price variation and affect all firms similarly. Once these global drivers of energy prices are controlled through the time dummies, the remaining variation in energy prices mostly reflects differences in domestic energy taxes or emission limits imposed on the energy sector (Sato et al., 2019[16]). It should be noted that firms are often able to negotiate firm-specific energy contracts, so that actual energy prices faced by firms might differ from sector-level energy prices used in the analysis. However, firm-specific energy prices would be endogenous in the estimation (because they are partly chosen by firms based on negotiations with utilities). The use of sector-specific energy prices helps to avoid this endogeneity.

Data

The dataset covers 30 OECD economies, 10 manufacturing sectors, spans the time period from 1995 to 2011 and consists of a total of (70 497 observations from 12 619 listed firms). The firm-level data are retrieved from Thomson Reuters Worldscope database, which compiles mandatory information from balance sheets and income statements on variables such as investment and sales. While the data are audited and thus very reliable, the dataset covers only listed firms, limiting the validity of the results to such firms. The investment figures in the dataset include investment in foreign subsidiaries, thus reflecting total investment. However, a sub-sample of the dataset also includes data on domestic investment, allowing to investigate whether effects of energy prices differ across domestic and foreign investment, shedding some light on the Pollution Haven Hypothesis (see Chapter 6 for an in-depth analysis of the Pollution Haven Hypothesis). The investment data from Worldscope are more volatile than economy-wide business investment data from the OECD STAN database, but are similar in level (and broad trends over time). Sector-specific data on energy prices are taken from Sato et al. (2019[16]). The prices are deflated and include taxes paid by industry but exclude VAT and other recoverable taxes and levies.

Results

Total investment goes down, but the effect is heterogeneous

The baseline results show support for a downsizing effect on investment. The results shown in Table 4.1 (column 1) show a statistically significant negative correlation between rising energy prices and total investment, and the control variables show the expected signs. These baseline results are, however, mainly driven by sectors that are not very energy intensive. Adding an interaction term between the sectors' energy-intensity and the change in energy prices allows investigation if there is a heterogeneous reaction of sectors. The results in Table 4.1 (column 2) show a statistically significant positive coefficient of the interaction term: the more energy-intensive the sectors are, the smaller the decrease in investment in response to higher energy prices. Figure 4.1 shows that very energy-intensive sectors even show an increase in investment in response to rising energy prices, possibly suggesting that these firms invest in more energy-efficient or abatement technologies.

Figure 4.1. Effect of higher energy prices on the investment ratio

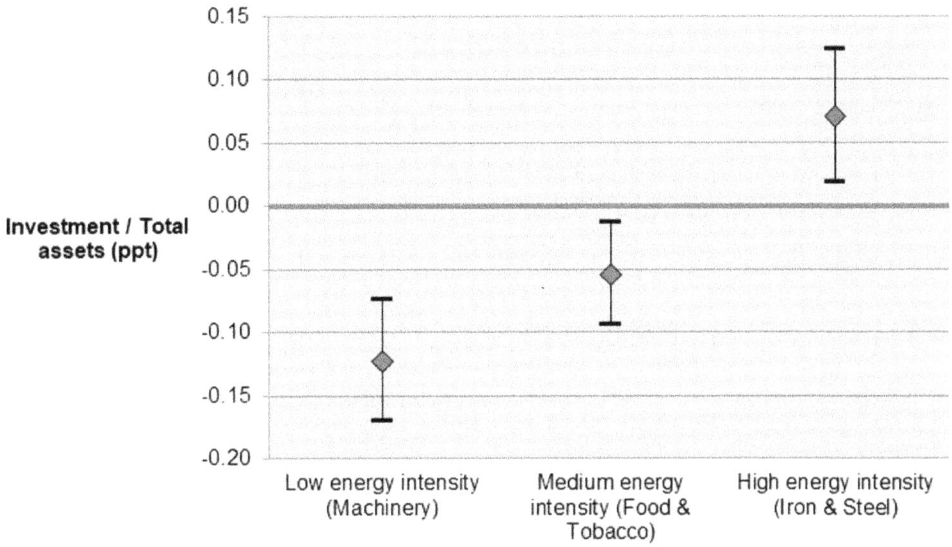

Note: The figure shows the effect on the investment ratio associated with energy price inflation equivalent to the 75th percentile of energy price growth within the sample. This is equivalent to the difference in energy price inflation between Poland and Germany over the sample period. The authors first order countries by their average energy price inflation over time and sectors. The baseline growth in energy prices is taken as the median growth in energy prices across countries, which is equivalent to the growth in energy prices in Poland in their sample. This baseline growth in energy prices is compared with a high energy prices growth, specifically the 75% percentile, which is equivalent to growth in German energy prices over the sample. The figure can be interpreted as showing the expected annual change in the average investment ratio of Polish firms, if energy prices over the sample were to rise as fast as in Germany. Low energy-intensity refers to the machinery sector, medium energy-intensity to the food and tobacco sector and high energy-intensity to the iron and steel sector. The centre point estimate is plotted together with the 95% confidence intervals. The results are based on Table 4.1 column 2.
Source: Dlugosch and Koźluk (2017[6]).

Policy-driven price increases seem to trigger investment effect

The effects of increased energy prices on investment are likely driven by tighter environmental policies in the up-stream sector. Energy prices might not be an optimal proxy for all environmental policies as they mainly reflect environmental policies in up-stream, energy-producing sectors. The OECD's Environmental Policy Stringency Index (EPS) is thus used to decompose the energy price inflation into a policy component, which covers price increases triggered by policy changes, and a residual component, which includes all other effects triggering price increases. This decomposition is done in two steps. First, the authors regress energy price inflation on EPS growth. In a second step they re-estimate their empirical model including both the policy-driven and the residual components of changes in energy prices as explanatory variables. The results show support for the hypothesis that the investment effect is indeed driven by changes in environmental up-stream policies (Table 4.1. , column 3).

Dirty sectors are more sensitive to price changes, particularly in times of high energy price levels

The effect on investment of changes in energy prices differs with the level of the energy prices (Table 4.1. , column 4). Adding an interaction term indicating whether the energy price in a certain year lies above the sector median energy prices or not, shows that the investment effect differs for low and high levels of energy prices. For low levels of energy prices, a change in energy prices is negatively correlated with investment for energy-efficient sectors, while they do not seem to react in times when energy prices are high. Energy-intensive sectors, on the other hand, only seem to react to rising energy prices, when the energy price level is already high.

Table 4.1. Investment effects - main estimation results

Dependent variable: Investment/total assets	(1)	(2)	(3)	(4)	(5)	(6)
	Baseline	Sector-level heterogeneity	Policy component	Level effects	Total investment where domestic available	Domestic investment
Energy Intensity * EPI Inflation (MA) $_{(t-1)}$		0.0872***			0.0648***	0.1252***
		(0.0141)			(0.0171)	(0.0402)
EPI (Inflation) (MA) $_{(t-1)}$	-0.0107*	-0.0132**			-0.0057	-0.0795***
	(0.0057)	(0.0057)			(0.0073)	(0.0216)
Energy Int. * EPI (Inflation) - Policy Part			0.0896***			
			(0.0146)			
EPI Inflation - Policy Part			-0.0108*			
			(0.0061)			
Energy Int. * EPI Inflation - Residual Part			0.0885***			
			(0.0142)			
EPI Inflation - Residual Part			-0.0114*			
			(0.0061)			
Low price level:				0.0931***		
Energy intensity * EPI Inflation (MA) $_{(t-1)}$				(0.0208)		
High price level:				0.0759***		
Energy intensity * EPI inflation (MA) $_{(t-1)}$				(0.0193)		
Low price level: EPI inflation (MA) $_{(t-1)}$				-0.0372***		
				(0.0067)		
High price level: EPI inflation (MA) $_{(t-1)}$				0.0160**		
				(0.0071)		
Observations	68,334	68,334	68,180	68,334	35,633	35,633
Adj. R2	0.412	0.413	0.4806	0.413	0.447	0.0574

Notes: All models include firm- and time fixed effects, sales over total capital, lagged out gap and lagged real interest rates, an interaction of lay-off rates and employment protection and a financial dependency control as further controls. Estimated coefficients of control variables are not shown. EPI inflation (MA) denotes the three-year moving average of changes in the energy price indicator. Energy-intensity is the share of electricity, water and gas inputs in total inputs to the production of each industry. Low and high levels are defined as being above or below the pooled median. The energy-intensity has been demeaned before application. Low energy-intensive sectors thus have a negative sign. Firm clustered standard errors in parentheses. *, **, *** denote significance at the 10, 5, and 1% level respectively.

Divestment effect of domestic investment is present for clean and dirty sectors

Re-estimating the equation for a sample of firms where total investment can be broken down into its domestic and foreign components confirms the heterogeneous effects on total investment in energy-intensive sectors. However, looking only at domestic investment, the differentiated effect among clean and dirty sectors vanishes and a negative effect of rising energy prices is found on domestic investment throughout all sectors (Chapter 1, Figure 1.8.). This suggests that firms in the overall sample tend to invest more abroad, which compensates for the decrease in domestic investment (see Chapter 6 for a more detailed analysis of the Pollution Haven Hypothesis).

Robustness checks

The results are robust to several additional checks. First, restricting the sample to the period before the financial crisis does not change the results, neither does an exclusion of US firms (as US firms represent one quarter of the sample). The results are also robust to adding country-year and sector-year fixed effects. The results also hold when estimating a dynamic (instead of a static) panel specification using a one-step system GMM estimator.

Conclusion

Energy-intensive sectors seem to offshore investment

This study finds that increasing energy prices are associated with lower total investment by firms listed on the stock market. However, this relationship differs among sectors with low and high energy-intensity. Low energy-intensive sectors show lower investment during times of increasing energy prices. Energy-intensive sectors show higher total investment when energy prices increase. These investment effects can be largely attributed to a tightening of up-stream environmental policies. One possible explanation for these results is the offshoring of investment by energy-intensive sectors. While results on domestic investment show a negative correlation with higher energy prices across all sectors, total investment in energy-intensive sectors seems to increase at the same time, hinting at more pronounced investment activities abroad.

Small firms not covered here might provide innovative technological solutions

It is important to keep the context of this study in mind when interpreting the results. The underlying sample consists only of listed (usually bigger and more established) firms. However, innovative technological solutions in response to tighter environmental policies might come from new entrants and SMEs, which are often not listed on the stock market and thus not covered in this analysis. Moreover, depreciation of capital is not considered in this study but could also be affected by more stringent environmental policies.

Additional policies might help to mitigate the estimated effect on investment

This study underlines the importance of considering general framework policies in addition to environmental policies. The results of this study show that environmental policies as such do not seem to foster investment among existing firms and might even reduce investment. However, by raising input (especially energy) costs, it is probable that these policies trigger investment in energy-saving capital on the one hand but reduce investment in other domains on the other hand, thus reducing total investment. While this study does not identify specific effects on energy-saving investments, policy makers should keep the crowding-out effect on investment in mind when considering environmental policies. Complementary policies, which reduce the cost of capital or improve general financing conditions without putting pressure on financial stability, can be helpful to mitigate such divestments.

Notes

[1] This chapter is a summary of the paper "Energy prices, environmental policies and investment – Evidence from listed firms" by D. Dlugosch and T. Koźluk, published as OECD Economics Department Working Paper No. 1378.

[2] More efficient production processes can reduce the environmental impact through at least three channels. First, processes can reduce the overall energy demand of firms, improving the energy efficiency. The carbon intensity of the energy savings determines the emission reductions. Second, firms can change energy sources for example by switching from carbon intensive coal to less carbon intensive natural gas or renewable sources of energy. This reduces the amount of carbon emissions per unit of output. Third, firms can reduce their non-energy related material inputs, for example the amount of raw materials used in production. Since the extraction, transportation and use of raw materials is often carbon intensive, improving the material efficiency can reduce carbon emissions and lower the overall environmental footprint of production.

References

Constantini, V. and E. Paglialunga (2014), "Elasticity of substition in capital-energy relationships: how central is a sector-based panel estimation approach", *SEEDS Working Paper*, Vol. 13/2014, http://www.sustainability-seeds.org/papers/RePec/srt/wpaper/1314.pdf. [5]

Dlugosch, D. and T. Koźluk (2017), "Energy prices, environmental policies and investment - evidence from listed firms", *OECD Economics Department Working Papers*, Vol. 1378, https://doi.org/10.1787/ef6c01c6-en. [6]

Gabaix, X. (2011), "The Granular Origins of Aggregate Fluctuations", *Econometrics*, Vol. 79/3, pp. 733-772, https://doi.org/10.3982/ECTA8769. [14]

Garofalo, G. and D. Malhotra (1995), "Effect of Environmental Regulations on State-level manufacturing capital formation", *Journal of Regional Science*, https://doi.org/10.1111/j.1467-9787.1995.tb01254.x. [11]

Gray, W. and R. Shadbegian (1998), "Environmental Regulation, Investment Timing, and Technology Choice", *The Journal of Industrial Economics*, pp. 235-256, https://www.jstor.org/stable/117550?seq=1#metadata_info_tab_contents. [12]

Greenstone, M. (2002), "The Impacts of Environmental Regulations on Industrial Activity: Evidence from the 1970 and 1977 Clean Air Act Amendments and the Census of Manufacturers", *Journal of Political Economy*, pp. 1175-1219, https://www.jstor.org/stable/10.1086/342808. [7]

Hamamoto, M. (2006), "Environmental regulation and the productivity of Japanese manufacturing industries", *Resource and energy economics*, Vol. 28/4, pp. 299-312, https://doi.org/10.1016/j.reseneeco.2005.11.001. [9]

Holly, S. and P. Smith (1989), "Interrelated Factor Demands for Manufacturing: A Dynamic Translog Cost Function Approach", *European Economic Review*, Vol. 33/1, pp. 111-126, https://doi.org/10.1016/0014-2921(89)90040-8. [15]

IPCC (2014), *Climate Change 2014: Synthesis Report. Contribution of Working Groups I, II, and III to the Fifth Assessment Report of the Intergovernmental Panel on Climate Change [Core Writing Team, R.K. Pachauri and L.A. Meyer (eds.)]]*. [1]

Kneller, R. and E. Manerson (2012), "Environmental regulations and innovation activity in UK manufacturing industries", *Resource and Energy Economics*, pp. 211-235, https://doi.org/10.1016/j.reseneeco.2011.12.001. [13]

Leiter, A., A. Parolini and H. Winner (2011), "Environmental regulation and investment: Evidence from European industry data", *Ecological Economics*, pp. 759-770, https://doi.org/10.1016/j.ecolecon.2010.11.013. [10]

McKinsey (2013), *Pathways to a Low-carbon Economy - Version 2 of the Global Greenhouse Gas Abatement Cost Curve*, https://www.mckinsey.com/business-functions/sustainability/our-insights/pathways-to-a-low-carbon-economy. [2]

Nelson, R., T. Tietenburg and M. Donihue (1993), "Differential Environmental Regulation: Effects on Electric Utility Capital Turnover and Emissions", *The Review of Economics and Statistics*, pp. 368-373, https://www.jstor.org/stable/pdf/2109447.pdf. [8]

OECD (2012), *OECD Environmental Outlook to 2050: The Consequences of Inaction*, OECD Publishing, Paris, https://dx.doi.org/10.1787/9789264122246-en. [3]

Sato, M. et al. (2019), "International and sectoral variation in industry energy prices 1995-2015", *Energy Economics*, Vol. 78, pp. 235-258. [16]

Xepapadeas, A. and A. de Zeeuw (1998), "Environmental Policy and Competitiveness: The Porter Hypothesis and the Composition of Capital", *Journal of Environmental Economics and Management*, pp. 165-182, https://doi.org/10.1006/jeem.1998.1061. [4]

5 Foreign direct investment and energy prices

Outward foreign direct investment (FDI) is the focus of this chapter.[1] Globally, foreign direct investment increased substantially over the past four decades, particularly in the manufacturing sector. This sector heavily depends on energy as a production input and could experience a loss in competitiveness when energy prices rise because of more stringent environmental regulation. This chapter investigates whether firms have redirected investment towards foreign countries with lower energy prices and laxer environmental policies, thereby shifting polluting emissions – a potential consequence of asymmetric environmental policies, known as the pollution haven effect. Empirical studies on this topic have so far mostly focused on outward FDI from a single country. This study sheds light on the relation between industrial energy prices and FDI flows in a cross-country setting. The effect of higher energy prices on firm-level outward FDI is estimated for a sample of 3 364 listed firms operating in nine manufacturing sectors across 24 OECD countries over the time period 1995-2008, using an instrumental variable method. The results show that higher domestic energy prices relative to energy prices abroad are indeed positively associated with the share of foreign assets firms hold. This effect is, however, small in magnitude. Moreover, while firms increase their share of foreign assets following an increase in domestic energy prices, a decrease in domestic energy prices is not followed by an increase in the share of domestic assets.

Background

Increases in FDI might be motivated by rising energy prices

Foreign direct investment (FDI) has gained more importance with the increasing global dimension of production processes over the past four decades as reported by, for example, UNCTAD. Investing in foreign assets might be beneficial to the investing firm in terms of improving the efficiency of its production lines and gaining access to the local market, while the host country might benefit from technology and know-how transfers as well as from economic development (De Mello, 1997[108]; Saggi, 2002[109]; see also OECD, 2002[110] for a survey). However, improving production patterns and accessing local demand might not be the only reasons for firms to invest abroad – they might want to circumvent tighter domestic environmental policies by shifting their production to countries with laxer regulations. Figure 5.1 shows the share of foreign assets over total assets for the sample of firms underlying this study over the period 1995-2008, along with the evolution of energy prices in the domestic market of these firms. As can be seen from Figure 5.1, both FDI and energy prices both rose from the early 2000s, suggesting that part of the rise in FDI could have been associated with off-shoring in the face of higher energy prices.

Figure 5.1. International assets as a share of total assets and average domestic energy prices, 1995-2008

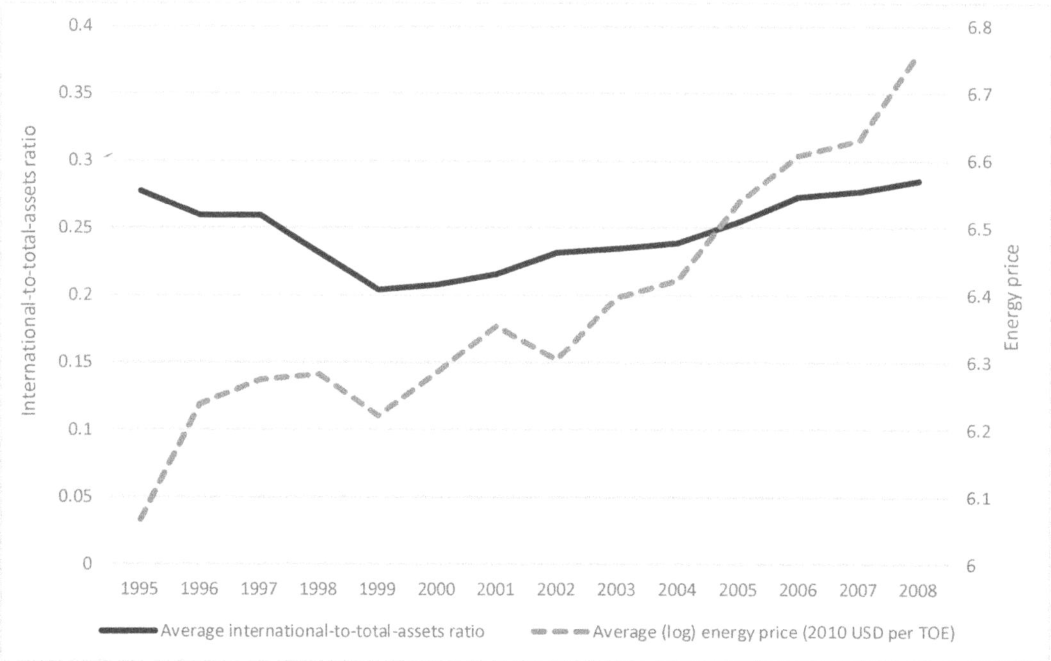

Note: Averages based on annual firm-level data. Energy prices are in real terms and shown in log.
Source: Garsous, Koźluk and Dlugosch (2020[1]).

Carbon leakage effect through FDI

The so-called pollution haven effect predicts that firms will respond to tighter domestic environmental policies by shifting production activity towards countries with less stringent environmental policies. Since countries with laxer environmental policies are predicted to gain a competitive advantage in heavily polluting industries (Pethig, 1976[2]; Siebert, 1977[3]; Yohe, 1979[4]), tighter environmental policies should provide incentives for firms to relocate parts of their production processes to countries with laxer regulations (Siebert, 1977[3]; McGuire, 1982[5]; Merrifield, 1988[6]). Assuming that capital is sufficiently mobile across countries, and transportation costs are not too high, this relocation effect is of particular concern for pollution-intensive industries when implementing new environmental regulations. It can lead to carbon leakage, whereby emissions are not reduced by new environmental regulations but simply shifted to other locations, which is a particular concern for global pollutants such as CO_2.

The empirical literature comprises mainly single country studies

The empirical evidence around the pollution haven effect has focused mostly on single country studies until now (see Garsous, Koźluk and Dlugosch (2020[1]) for a detailed review of the literature and Rezza, (2015[7]), for a meta-analysis). This focus is often data-driven, as is probably the geographical focus on the United States. Moreover, the literature is inconclusive so far, with results varying from significant effects (Hanna, 2010[8]; Chung, 2014[9]), to no effects (Eskeland and Harrison, 2003[10]; Kirkpatrick and Shimamoto, 2008[11]; Manderson and Kneller, 2012[12]). Other studies find that the effects vary with, for example, the ability to relocate (Kellenberg, 2009[13]; Cole and Elliott, 2005[14]), the host country's characteristics (Ben Kheder and Zugravu, 2012[15]) or the firm's home country characteristics (Dean, Lovely and Wang, 2009[16]). However, the proxies for environmental regulation vary across studies, as does the definition of the FDI variable, which could potentially account for the different effects found in the studies.

The first cross-country study, accounting for endogenous firm choice of fuel inputs

This study offers three main contributions to the literature. First, it provides the first cross-country analysis on the relationship between energy prices and FDI at the firm level. Second, the use of energy prices as a proxy for environmental policies, allowing for a better understanding of various environmental policies compared to previous studies, which focuses on pollution abatement costs. Most climate and air pollution policies ultimately affect energy prices – be it directly through additional taxes, or cap-and-trade systems, or indirectly through command-and-control mechanisms – making it a valuable proxy. Third, this study addresses endogeneity concerns about firms' choices of fuel substitution by using an instrumental variable approach to remove the effects of firms' substitution choices from the effect of observed energy prices.

Empirical set-up

Absolute versus relative energy price changes

The pollution haven effect predicts that it is the *difference* between the investors' and the receiving country's energy prices which drive FDI patterns, rather than changes in the domestic energy prices per se. Therefore, this study uses changes in *relative prices* as the main explanatory variable. The relative price changes are proxied by taking the difference in domestic energy prices and energy prices in China in the same sector.[2] China is the country that had the lowest energy prices over estimation period and was an increasingly important destination country for FDI. In addition, the study also tests whether changes in domestic energy prices directly trigger investments abroad.

An instrumental variable approach is used to avoid endogeneity problems in the estimation

There might be industry-level factors which influence both FDI patterns and trends in energy prices, leading to potential endogeneity problems in the estimation of the effects. Technological changes or industry-level shocks to output demand might affect the distribution of industry fuel demand, and consequently energy prices (Linn, 2008[17]). At the same time, these factors might influence FDI decisions of firms, for example, a new clean technology becoming available might make firms rely on a particular fuel more, while at the same time delaying investment in international assets. To avoid such an endogeneity bias, this study follows Linn (2008[17]) and Sato and Dechezleprêtre (2015[18]) by using as an instrumental variable sector-specific energy prices which are weighted according to time-invariant proportions of fuel used at the sector-level. Using these constant weights removes effects of technological change or other industry-specific shocks from the observed energy prices.

Empirical model

This analysis focuses on long-term impacts of changes in energy prices on outward FDI flows by estimating long-differences equations: the first and last observation for each firm are used to estimate the equation below. This implies that short-run effects of variations in energy prices will not be captured in the analysis. The following equation is estimated using a two-stage least squares within estimator:

$$\log(FDI)_{ijct} = \alpha + \beta \log(EP)_{jct} + \gamma X_{ijct} + \mu_i + \lambda_{ct} + \varepsilon_{ijct}$$

where FDI_{ijct} are the international assets of firm i in sector j in country c at time t. The FDI variable is defined as for-profit assets held by a firm which can be priced. EP_{jct} is, depending on the estimation, either the domestic energy price for sector j, constructed by weighting country-level fuel prices (oil, gas, coal and electricity) by their relative consumption in each country-sector-year, instrumented by fixed-weights energy prices as described above, or the relative energy price difference of country c with regard to Chinese energy prices, instrumented by the difference in fixed-weight prices. X_{ijct} is a set of firm-level control variables including firm size measured as number of employees, total assets and international sales as a measure of international openness. μ_i is a firm fixed-effect, λ_{ct} is a country-year dummy which controls country-specific effects such as institutional settings at the country level, and ε_{ijct} is the idiosyncratic error term.

Data

The dataset is an unbalanced panel from 1995 to 2008 which covers 3 364 firms, operating in 24 OECD economies and 9 different manufacturing sectors. The firm-level data are taken from the Thomson Reuters Worldscope database, which provides balance sheet information about listed firms. Only firms, which are already engaged in FDI are part of the analysis. The data on energy prices are taken from Sato et al. (2019[19]) , who provide a fixed-weight index of energy prices (based on weights from the baseline year 1995).

Results

Relative energy prices are a driver of FDI as opposed to absolute prices

The main results show that relative prices matter for FDI flows, while there is no statistically significant effect detected for absolute prices alone. Table 5.1. shows the main results of the estimation where the coefficient of the domestic energy price variable is insignificant, while the coefficient of the difference between domestic and Chinese energy prices is significantly positive. An increase of the relative energy price of 1% is estimated to be associated with a 0.5% increase in firms' international assets. The coefficients of the control variables are also significant and of expected sign, supporting the suitability of the estimated model.

Table 5.1. FDI effects - main estimation results

Dependent variable: International assets (log)	Absolute energy prices (1)	Relative energy prices (2)	Absolute energy prices (3)	Relative energy prices (4)
Domestic energy price (log)	0.625			
	(0.481)			
Relative energy price (= log domestic energy price – log Chinese energy price)		0.510**		
		(0.259)		
Energy price (log) * Dummy for increasing energy prices			0.613	
			(0.483)	
Energy price (log) * Dummy for decreasing energy prices			0.659	
			(0.500)	
Relative energy price (log) * Dummy for increasing domestic energy prices				0.711**
				(0.326)
Relative energy price (log) * Dummy for decreasing domestic energy prices				0.412
				(0.302)
Country-year fixed effects	YES	YES	YES	YES
Number of observations	6,728	6,728	6,728	6,728
Number of firms	3,364	3,364	3,364	3,364
R-squared	0.312	0.315	0.312	0.314

Notes: Column 1 uses the FEPL index from Sato et al. (2019[19]) as an instrument for observed energy prices. Column 2 uses relative prices as measured by the difference between domestic and Chinese prices. The differences between the domestic and Chinese FEPL index from Sato et al. (2019[19]) is used as an instrument for observed relative prices. Column 3 and 4 use interaction terms, indicating whether the firm faced an energy price increase or decrease over the observation period. All estimations include the size of firm, total assets and international sales as additional control variables. The coefficient estimates are not shown here for reasons of brevity. Robust standard errors clustered at the country-sector level in parentheses: ***, ** and * represent $p<0.01$, $p<0.05$, $p<0.1$ respectively.

Firms respond differently depending on whether they face an increase or decrease in energy prices

Firms might react to different energy price scenarios in different ways. While an increase in absolute or relative energy prices might incentivise firms to invest more in assets abroad, a decrease in energy prices might not immediately lead firms to withdraw their investments abroad. To study this hypothesis, the energy price variable is interacted with a dummy variable indicating whether the firm faced an increase or a decrease in energy prices over the observation period. The results in Table 5.1. (column 3 and 4) show that relative price changes are significantly positively associated with FDI only in the case of energy price increases, but not statistically significantly so for decreases. A 1% increase in relative energy prices is associated with a 0.7% increase in international assets by firms.

The economic magnitude of the effect is small

Only a very high carbon tax would be able to influence FDI patterns in an economically significant way. Using a back-of-the-envelope calculation, this study evaluates the effect of the implementation of a high carbon price in developed countries. It assumes that energy prices only rise in countries implementing the carbon tax. A low and a high carbon tax scenario is evaluated. The low carbon tax scenario, based on a carbon tax of USD 15/tonne CO_2, would increase energy prices by 5% on average, which would translate into an increase of 0.74 percentage points in the ratio of foreign assets to total assets. The higher carbon tax scenario relies on a carbon tax of USD 55/tonne CO_2 and would be expected to raise energy prices by 20% on average for the sample, translating into an increase of 2.6 percentage points in the FDI ratio. As Figure 5.2 shows, these estimated changes in the FDI ratio are rather small compared to the baseline level of the FDI ratio. The calculations have to be taken with a grain of salt, however, as they are based on average effect estimates and rely on a range of other assumptions.

Figure 5.2. Simulated effect of unilateral carbon tax on outward FDI

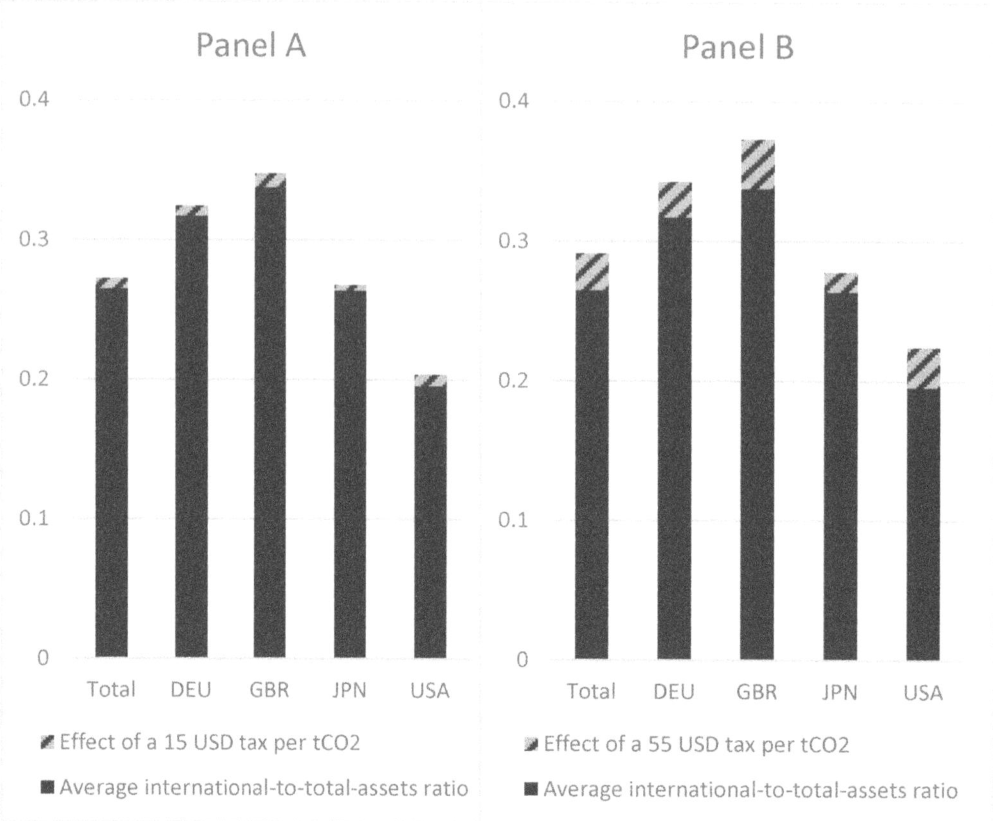

Note: These figures report the simulated effect of the introduction of a carbon tax on the international-to-total-asset ratio for the whole sample as well as for selected countries. Panel A shows a low carbon tax scenario (USD 15/tonne of CO_2), Panel B shows a higher carbon tax scenario (USD 55/tonne of CO_2).

Conclusion

Support for the pollution haven effect found – but magnitude is small

The results of this study show that relative energy prices (i.e. the difference between domestic energy prices and foreign energy prices) matter as a driver of FDI, but the magnitude of the effect is small. The effect is only found for firms facing an energy price increase at home, while a reduction in domestic energy prices is not correlated with a lower amount of international assets. For those firms which did see energy prices rise in their home country, a 1% increase in relative energy prices was associated with an increase of 0.71% in the firms' international assets. With an average share of international over total assets of 27% in the sample, this average effect on international assets is small.

The sample is limited to listed firms, and only the intensive margin is studied

These results are based on a specific sample of firms, namely firms which are listed on the stock market. While these firms are often larger, thus more engaged in international trade, and contribute a large part in explaining overall changes in the economy, this study is not able to make inferences about smaller companies. However, given that those firms already possess assets across various jurisdictions, they should be in theory the most inclined to undertake foreign investment and international relocation. Therefore, it is reasonable to assume that the effects should be smaller for smaller, less internationally exposed companies not covered in this study. It is also not possible to infer from this analysis whether firms, which did not already engage in FDI at all, will invest abroad because of higher energy prices since this study only covers firms which already engage in FDI.

Carbon leakage concerns are likely to be overstated

The simulation undertaken in the context of this analysis reveals that only a high carbon price would have an economically meaningful effect on the share of international assets held by firms. While the analysis relies on a carbon price of USD 55 /tonne of CO_2, the OECD has used a carbon price of USD 34/tonne of CO_2 as lower bound estimate of the social costs of carbon (OECD, 2015[20]; OECD, 2015[21]). If governments would agree to implement a carbon tax equal to the social costs of carbon or even above, this would, based on the results of this study, only have limited effects in terms of carbon leakage through foreign direct investment.

Notes

[1] This chapter is a summary of the paper "Do energy prices drive outward FDI? Evidence from a sample of listed firms" (2020[1]) by G. Garsous, T. Koźluk and D. Dlugosch, *The Energy Journal,* Vol. 41/3. An earlier version of this paper was published as the OECD Working Paper "Foreign Direct Investment and The Pollution Haven Hypothesis: Evidence from Listed Firms" by G. Garsous and T. Koźluk (2017[22]), OECD Economics Department Working Paper, No. 1379.

[2] The energy price data is deflated and converted to constant 2010 USD for tonnes of oil equivalent (toe).

References

Ben Kheder, S. and N. Zugravu (2012), "Environmental regulation and French firms location abroad: An economic geography model in an international comparative study", *Ecological Economics*, pp. 48-61, https://doi.org/10.1016/j.ecolecon.2011.10.005. [15]

Chung, S. (2014), "Environmental regulation and foreign direct investment: Evidence from South Korea", *Journal of Development Economics*, Vol. 108, pp. 222-236, https://doi.org/10.1016/j.jdeveco.2014.01.003. [9]

Cole, M. and R. Elliott (2005), "FDI and the Capital Intensity of "Dirty" Sectors: A Missing Piece of the Pollution Haven Puzzle", *Review of Development Economics*, Vol. 9, pp. 530-548, https://doi.org/10.1111/j.1467-9361.2005.00292.x. [14]

Dean, J., M. Lovely and H. Wang (2009), "Are foreign investors attracted to weak environmental regulations? Evaluating the evidence from China", *Journal of Development Economics*, Vol. 90, pp. 1-13, https://doi.org/10.1016/j.jdeveco.2008.11.007. [16]

Eskeland, G. and A. Harrison (2003), "Moving to greener pastures? Multinational and the Pollution Haven Hypothesis", *Journal of Development Economics*, Vol. 70, pp. 1-23, https://doi.org/10.1016/S0304-3878(02)00084-6. [10]

Garsous, G. and T. Kozluk (2017), "Foreign Direct Investment and The Pollution Haven Hypothesis - Evidence from Listed Firms", *OECD Economics Department Working Papers*, Vol. 1379, https://doi.org/10.1787/1e8c0031-en. [22]

Garsous, G., T. Koźluk and D. Dlugosch (2020), "Do energy prices drive outwards FDI? Evidence from a sample of listed firms", *The Energy Journal*, Vol. 41/3, http://dx.doi.org/doi:10.5547/01956574.41.3.ggar. [1]

Hanna, R. (2010), "US Environmental Regulation and FDI: Evidence from a Panel of US-Based Multinational Firms", *American Economic Journal: Applied Economics*, Vol. 2, pp. 158-189, https://www.aeaweb.org/articles?id=10.1257/app.2.3.158. [8]

Kellenberg, D. (2009), "An empirical investigation of the pollution haven effect with strategic environment and trade policy", *Journal of International Economics*, Vol. 78, pp. 242-255, https://doi.org/10.1016/j.jinteco.2009.04.004. [13]

Kirkpatrick, C. and K. Shimamoto (2008), "The effect of environmental regulation on the locational choice of Japanese foreign direct investment", *Applied Economics*, Vol. 30, pp. 1399-1409, https://doi.org/10.1080/00036840600794330. [11]

Linn, J. (2008), "Energy Prices and the Adoption of Energy-Saving Technology", *The Economic Journal*, Vol. 118, pp. 1986-2012, https://doi.org/10.1111/j.1468-0297.2008.02199.x. [17]

Manderson, E. and R. Kneller (2012), "Environmental Regulations, Outward FDI and Heterogeneous Firms: Are Countries used as Pollution Havens?", *Environmental and Resource Economics*, pp. 317-352, https://link.springer.com/article/10.1007/s10640-011-9500-z. [12]

McGuire, M. (1982), "Regulation, factor rewards, and international trade", *Journal of Public Economics*, Vol. 17/3, https://www.sciencedirect.com/science/article/pii/004727278290069X (accessed on 17 January 2019). [5]

Merrifield, J. (1988), "The impact of selected abatement strategies on transnational pollution, the terms of trade, and factor rewards: A general equilibrium approach", *Journal of Environmental Economics and Management*, Vol. 15, pp. 259-284, https://doi.org/10.1016/0095-0696(88)90002-2. [6]

OECD (2015), *Effective Carbon Rates on Energy*, OECD Publishing, Paris, https://www.oecd.org/tax/tax-policy/effective-carbon-rates-2018-brochure.pdf. [21]

OECD (2015), *Taxing Energy Use 2015: OECD and Selected Partner Economies*, OECD Publishing, Paris, https://dx.doi.org/10.1787/9789264232334-en. [20]

Pethig, R. (1976), "Pollution, welfare, and environmental policy in the theory of comparative advantage", *Journal of Environmental Economics and Management*, Vol. 2, pp. 160-169, https://doi.org/10.1016/0095-0696(76)90031-0. [2]

Rezza, A. (2015), "A meta-analysis of FDI and environmental regulations", *Environment and Development Economics*, Vol. 20/2015, pp. 185-208, https://doi.org/10.1017/S1355770X14000114. [7]

Sato, M. and A. Dechezleprêtre (2015), "Asymmetric industrial energy prices and international trade", *Energy Economics*, Vol. 52, pp. S130-S141, http://dx.doi.org/10.1016/J.ENECO.2015.08.020. [18]

Sato, M. et al. (2019), "International and sectoral variation in industry energy prices 1995-2015", *Energy Economics*, Vol. 78, pp. 235-258. [19]

Siebert, H. (1977), "Environmental quality and the gains from trade", *Kyklos*, Vol. 30, pp. 657-673, http://hdl.handle.net/10419/3530. [3]

Yohe, G. (1979), "The backward incidence of pollution control - some comparative statics in general equilibrium", *Journal of Environmental Economics and Management*, Vol. 6, pp. 187-198, https://doi.org/10.1016/0095-0696(79)90002-0. [4]

6 Global value chains, environmental policies, and the Pollution Haven hypothesis

Global value chains are the focus of this chapter.[1] The increased fragmentation of production chains around the globe over the last decades, paired with varying efforts of environmental protection across countries, have reinforced fears of policy makers that industrial activity may shift towards jurisdictions with laxer environmental policies – an argument known as the Pollution Haven hypothesis. The empirical evidence on this hypothesis has focused on aggregate trade patterns so far. Using data on gross exports and domestic value added of exports in the manufacturing sector across 23 OECD and 6 BRIICS countries over the period 1990-2009, this study assesses how trade patterns are related to differences in national environmental policies of trading partners based on a gravity model of bilateral trade flows. The results of the study show that an increasing difference between the domestic and the trading partners' environmental policy stringency does not alter overall trade but it does affect the specialisation of countries: tighter environmental policies in one country are linked to a comparative disadvantage in dirty industries and a comparative advantage in cleaner industries. These effects are, however, small in magnitude, when compared with other policies such as trade liberalisation measures.

Background

The increased fragmentation of production chains gives rise to global value chains

While traditional trade theory identified countries' factor endowments, i.e. labour, capital, institutions and natural capital, as a main driver of trade patterns, the past two decades have shown an increasing importance of specialised stages of the production process. Therefore, in recent trade models, the focus has shifted towards the fragmented production process along global value chains (GVCs), which exploit differences in factor endowments and efficiencies across jurisdictions and thereby lead to different stages of specialisation (Baldwin and Yan, 2014[1]). A comparative advantage of one country over another is thus not always associated with the sale of finished goods and services but rather with specialised intermediate goods and services.

The comparative advantage of economies might be shifted by tighter environmental policies

Increasing environmental protection efforts might lead to a change of comparative production advantages across economies. Environmental policies might implicitly or explicitly increase the cost of using the environment as a production factor and require firms to invest some of their production inputs into pollution mitigation and abatement. Given that the stringency of environmental policies differ heavily across countries, the relative costs of environmental inputs differ across countries as well, potentially affecting the comparative advantage of economies in the production of certain goods and services. Tighter environmental policies may increase the relative cost advantage of economies towards cleaner production, thereby potentially putting polluting domestic firms at a competitive disadvantage. Separating effects for BRIICS and OECD countries, Figure 6.1 shows that dirty sectors indeed have a higher export share in countries with less stringent environmental policies. Whether this is a simple coincidence or whether environmental policies triggered these patterns, is the subject of this analysis.

Figure 6.1. Export shares by sector-specific environmental dependence across country groups and different levels of EPS

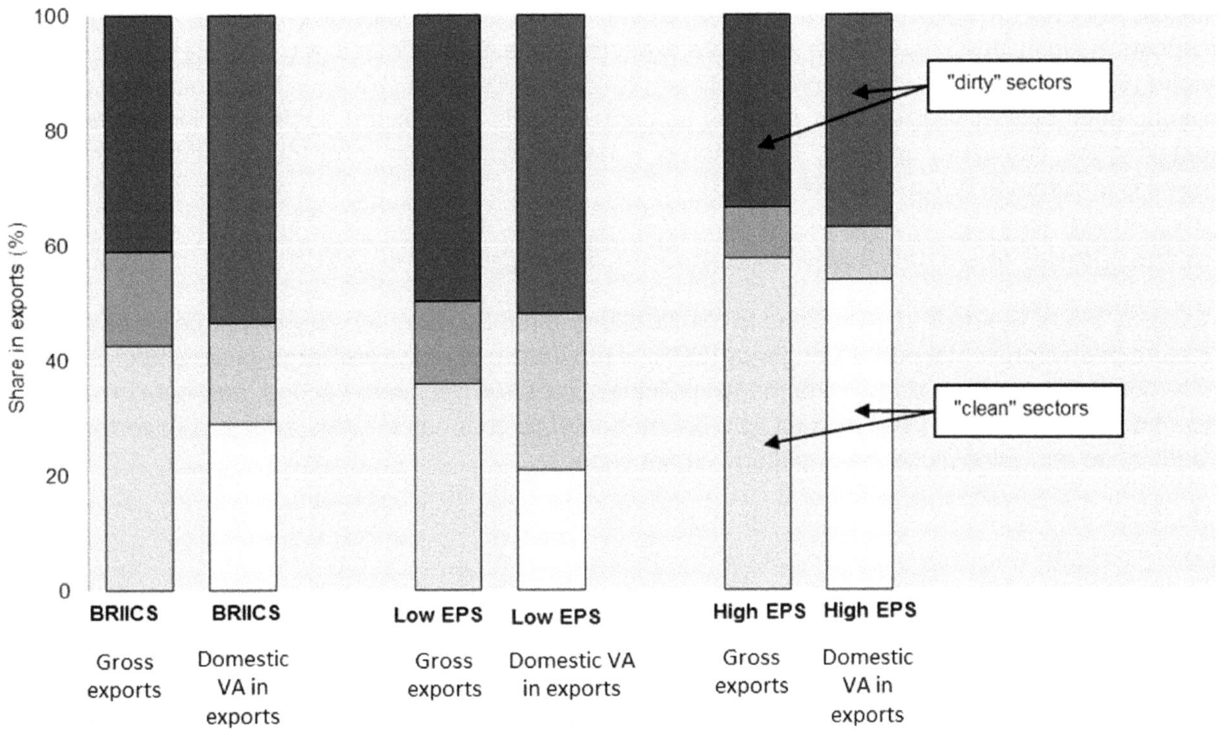

Notes: The figure shows the share of exports (domestic VA in exports and gross exports) of three industry groups, by pollution intensity: "dirty" (4 sectors with highest pollution intensity), "medium" (2 sectors with average pollution intensity) and "clean" (4 sectors with lowest pollution intensity). Averages over the sample 1995-2008 are reported. Countries are grouped into BRIICS (generally lowest EPS), low EPS (OECD countries with lowest average EPS across the sample: Australia, Ireland and the Slovak Republic) and high EPS (OECD countries with highest EPS across the sample: Denmark, Germany and Switzerland).
Source: Koźluk and Timiliotis (2016[2]).

Offshoring versus efficiency gains – what the theory says

A priori, it is unclear whether and how firms will adjust their production chains in response to more stringent environmental policies. On the one hand, environmental policies which increase input costs might provide incentives for offshoring certain production stages to countries with laxer environmental policies along the lines of the Pollution Haven Hypothesis (PHH) (McGuire, 1982[3]). Additionally, these policies might incentivise sourcing carbon-intensive inputs from other countries and thereby affect trade patterns. On the other hand, tighter environmental policies might lead to a re-design of production processes whereby efficiency potentials might be discovered, an argument known as the Porter Hypothesis (Porter, 1991[4]; Porter and van der Linde, 1995[5]). Reaping efficiency and productivity gains in response to environmental policies might increase the competitiveness of firms and provide them with a comparative advantage in cleaner production processes.

Empirical studies so far ignored changes in the domestic part of value added in exports

The link between GVCs and environmental policies has not been studied in depth until now. While there is an extensive literature on the link between environmental policies and trade (see Koźluk and Timiliotis (2016[2]) for a detailed review), the empirical evidence around GVCs has been limited so far. The majority of studies investigating the PHH have used gross or net trade flows, thereby ignoring effects on the domestic value added part of exports. One notable exception is a study by Kellenberg (2009[6]) which finds support for the PHH for value added in affiliates of US-owned multinationals. Studies focusing on gross or net trade flows mostly use gravity models of trade behaviour, often augmented with factor endowments and policy-related drivers of trade. While some papers look at overall competitiveness, the majority focuses on effects in highly polluting sectors, which are expected to be most affected (e.g. Van Beers and van den Bergh (1997[7]); Ederington, Levinson and Minier (2005[8]); Kellenberg (2009[6]). The choice of a proxy for environmental policies ranges from pollution abatement costs over expert surveys to indicators directly measuring the stringency of policy instruments. However, conducting robustness checks with several proxies is uncommon in the literature so far.

Contribution of this study - new evidence on domestic part of GVCs

This study offers two main contributions to the literature. First, by using a newly developed cross-country measure of environmental policy stringency (EPS), it provides one of the first large-scale empirical studies on the link between GVCs and environmental policies across two decades. Second, new data on domestic value added in exports is used to shed light on the domestic changes in value added to exported goods, in addition to analysing global trade patterns in net exports.

Empirical set-up

An augmented gravity model is deployed

The empirical analysis is based on a gravity model of bilateral trade, augmented with variables explaining competitive differences across countries. Gravity models have been extensively used in the trade literature (e.g. McCallum, (1995[9]); Frankel (1997[10]); Frankel and Rose (2002[11])) and have recently been augmented with variables explaining competitiveness differences in the vein of the Heckscher-Ohlin model (e.g. legal institutions in Nuun (2007[12]); financial development in Manova (2013[13]); Nicoletti et al. (2003[14])). One of these "policy-related endowments" added in this study is the stringency of environmental policies.

Data on the domestic share of value added provide a detailed look at GVCs

The empirical analysis examines the impact of environmental policy stringency on the traditional measure of trade between countries, net exports, as well as on the domestic share of value added in exports. While trade in intermediate goods was proportional to trade in final goods for a long time, the increasing appearance of global value chains altered this relationship (Yi, 2003[15]). Domestic environmental policies are expected to have a stronger effect on the domestic value added in production and exports than simply on gross exports which, to a large share, include imported intermediate components. It is therefore important to differentiate how much domestic value added lies in the exported goods in order to identify a more accurate relationship between environmental policies and trade patterns.

Heterogeneous sector effects

The analysis allows for heterogeneous sector- and production-stage effects. The environmental policy variable is only observed at the country-level. However, sectors might be more or less sensitive to changes in these policies. Therefore, the effects of environmental policy stringency are allowed to vary with the pollution intensity of sectors – assuming that pollution-intensive sectors may be subject to stronger effects of environmental policies (similar approaches are used by Rajan and Zingales (1998[16]); Johansson et al. (2014[17]); and Albrizio, Koźluk and Zipperer (2017[18]), summarised in Chapter 2). Furthermore, effects of tariffs are allowed to vary across intermediate and final goods. Following Johansson et al., (2014[17]), an input and output tariff variable is constructed, capturing the fact that intermediate goods tend to be more vulnerable to trade barriers than final goods because they are more easily substituted (Miroudot, Lanz and Ragoussis, 2009[19]).

Empirical model

Given the significant share of zero trade flows between countries in the dataset, a Poisson Pseudo Maximum Likelihood estimator is used to estimate the following equation:

$$\begin{aligned} Exp_{ijst} = \exp(&\alpha + \gamma_1 Gravity_{ijt} + \beta_1 Endowment_{it} * Intensity_s + \beta_2 Endowment_{jt} * Intensity_s \\ &+ \beta_3 Policy_{it} * Sensitivity_s + \beta_4 Policy_{jt} * Sensitivity_s + \delta_1 Endowment_{it} \\ &+ \delta_2 Policy_{it} + \delta_3 Endowment_{jt} + \delta_4 Policy_{jt} + \gamma_2 InputTariff_{sit} \\ &+ \gamma_3 OutputTariff_{sijt} + \lambda_1 EPSgap_{ijt} + \lambda_2 EPSgap_{ijt} * ED_s + \theta_i + \theta_j + \theta_s + \theta_t) \\ &+ \varepsilon_{ijst} \end{aligned}$$

where i is the exporting country, j is the importing country, s is the sector and t is the year. In the first analysis, Exp_{ijst} is the USD value of total gross manufacturing exports from country *i* to country *j* in year *t* in sector *s*; in the second analysis, Exp_{ijst} is the domestic value added in *i*'s exports to j. $Gravity_{ijt}$ is a set of gravity variables commonly used in such models such as geographical distance between capitals, GDP of each of the partner countries, dummies for the existence of a common border, common language, participation of both countries in a regional trade agreement, or a common currency. $Endowment$ is a set of country-level variables reflecting the endowments of the country with production factors such as the stock of physical capital per worker, human capital per worker and energy supply per capita. These variables are included for both trading partners and interacted with the variable $Intensity_s$ which measures the intensity with which the production factors are used in industry *s*. $Policy$ reflects policy and institutional variables, such as financial development and institutional quality. The policy variable is included for both trading partners and interacted with $Sensitivity_s$ which measures the dependence of a given sector on the respective policy variable. $InputTariff_{sit}$ is a weighted average of tariffs on intermediate goods imported into country *i* and used in sector *s*. $OutputTariff_{sijt}$ is a measure of average tariffs that importer *j* imposes on products of industry *s*. $EPSgap_{ijt}$ reflects the difference in the environmental policy stringency between country *i* and country *j*. This is interacted with ED_s, the environmental dependence of sector *s* on environmental policies, a sensitivity proxy which measures the industry pollution-intensity of sector *s*. $\theta_i, \theta_j, \theta_s, \theta_t$ are fixed effects for the importing country, the exporting country, the sector and the year. ε_{ijst} is the error term.

Data

The dataset is an unbalanced panel, which covers 23 OECD economies and 6 BRIICS countries, 10 manufacturing sectors, and spans the time period from 1990 to 2009. The data on gross imports are taken from the OECD STAN database, the EPS estimates are also taken from the OECD. The gravity variables are sourced from the CEPII database, CIA World Factbook, the WTO, De Sousa (2012[20]). The endowment and sensitivity variables are from Kowalski (2011[21]), Barro and Lee (2010[22]), World Bank, GTAP database, tariff data from Most Favourite Nation database and GTAP (see Koźluk and Timiliotis (2016[2]) for a detailed description of the variables and the respective sources).

Results

Only dirty sectors move part of gross exports to pollution havens

The results for gross exports show no support for the PHH at the country-level, but significant heterogeneous effects across sectors. When using gross manufacturing exports as the dependent variable, no significant effect of the EPS indicator is found, as shown in Table 6.1. However, when interacting the EPS variable with environmental dependence to allow for heterogeneous effects across sectors, a statistically significant negative effect is found for the difference in environmental policy stringency on trade patterns. The estimates for the other coefficients are in line with previous findings, but not shown here for the sake of brevity and can be found in Koźluk and Timiliotis (2016[2]). Calculating marginal effects for dirty and clean sectors reveals that for sectors where environmental policies are more stringent in the exporting country, exports of dirty sectors are significantly lower than in the case when environmental policies are equally stringent in both countries (Figure 6.2). For a difference of 0.42 in the EPS variable (which equals moving from the median to the 75th percentile of the EPS distribution), exports are 4% lower than in the case where both trading partners have equal levels of EPS. Similarly, when the exporting country has laxer environmental policies, exports of dirty sectors tend to be higher compared to the case, when environmental policy stringency is similar. Effects for clean sectors are not significant. These results suggest that countries face a comparative disadvantage in gross exports in dirty sectors when their domestic environmental efforts are stronger than the ones of their trading partners.

Table 6.1. Global value chain effects - main estimation results

Dependent variable:	Gross exports (in logs)		Domestic VA in exports (TiVA)	
	(1)	(2)	(3)	(4)
EPSgap	-0.0183	-0.0230	0.00364	0.00188
	(0.0166)	(0.0163)	(0.0284)	(0.0282)
EPSgap*ED		-0.142***		-0.362***
		(0.0366)		(0.0616)
Fixed effects (Exporter, importer, industry, year)	Yes	Yes	Yes	Yes
Pseudo R-squared	0.850	0.850	0.841	0.842
Observations	121 240	121 240	32 480	32 480

Notes: Robust standard errors in parentheses. ***, ** and * represent p<0.01, p<0.05, p<0.1 respectively.

The domestic share of value added is affected for both dirty and clean sectors

The results of the estimation based on domestic value added in exports additionally show a positive significant effect for clean sectors. The results shown in column 3 and 4 in Table 6.1. confirm the results found previously. However, as Figure 6.2 shows, next to the negative effect for dirty sectors, clean sectors see a positive impact on their domestic value added in exports when environmental policy stringency is high in the exporting country. If the environmental policy stringency is lower in the exporting country, then the value added in clean domestic sectors declines.

Figure 6.2. Marginal effects of environmental dependence on exports

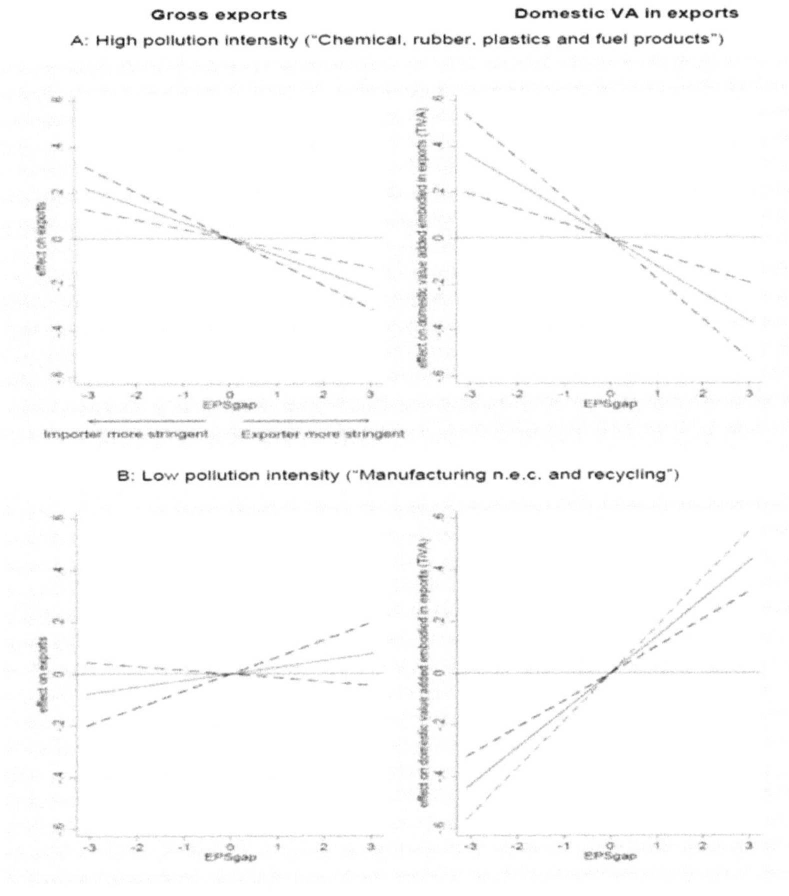

Note: 90% confidence intervals reported.

Economic significance for the domestic share of exports is larger than for net exports but the overall effect is small compared to other trade determinants

The economic significance of the results is higher for the domestic value added in exports than for gross exports, but small compared to other trade determinants. The initial hypothesis that environmental policies have a stronger impact on the domestic part of global value chains is confirmed in the analysis that compares the magnitude of the effects from the two estimations. When comparing the economic significance of the effects of environmental policy stringency to other trade determinants, the effect appears limited: The effects of a change in the EPS variable from the median to the 75th percentile would be equivalent to an 8% increase in output tariffs for dirty sector.

Robustness checks

The results are robust to several robustness checks. First, using energy prices taken from Sato et al. (2019[23]) as an alternative measure of environmental policies does not change the results significantly, neither does using the in-sample energy intensity of industries rather than pre-sample pollution intensity as sensitivity proxy. Using the sector's stage in the GVC in terms of being up- or downstream as an alternative proxy of environmental dependency does not alter the results significantly either. Second, using a lag of the EPS variable confirms the results of the contemporaneous estimation, showing an even stronger effect. Third, the results are robust to different specifications of the fixed effects structure, estimation based on different country and year sub-samples, and on alternative specifications of the gravity model.

Conclusion

Dirty industries face a competitive disadvantage, clean industries a competitive advantage

The findings of this study show no support for the PHH for aggregate trade, but they show evidence that environmental policies induce changes in specialisation across countries, in line with the PHH. The baseline results show no significant effect of tighter environmental policy on overall trade patterns in manufacturing goods. However, the country-specific stringency of environmental policies has a significant effect on the specialisation of firms, confirming the PHH. When the gap in environmental policy stringency between two trade partners increases, relative input prices change and the country with tighter environmental policies seems to suffer from a comparative disadvantage in "dirty" industries, while laxer environmental policies are associated with a new comparative advantage in "clean" industries. These effects are stronger for the domestic value added in exports than for total gross exports. While these specialisation effects are present, the analysis shows that these changes in trade patterns are small when compared to changes induced by, for example, trade liberalisation measures.

The detailed design of environmental policies is not captured

The role of the design of environmental policies has to be kept in mind when interpreting the results. The measure used in this study for environmental policy stringency can only be seen as a general proxy. It fails to capture details of the design of policy instruments, especially exemption rules for high-polluting sectors. These exemptions can sometimes hamper innovations and investments, delaying a shift towards cleaner production.

A good policy setting could help clean sectors gain competitiveness

An adequate policy setting may help economies foster growth in "clean" sectors. The extent to which environmental policies influence bilateral trade patterns and the comparative advantage of economies depends on the ability of the economies to shift resources from losing sectors to cleaner and innovative sectors. This ability is often influenced by general economic policy settings in the countries. Implementing suitable policy settings, which support the switch from dirty to clean sectors can thus help achieving environmental objectives and potentially create a first-mover advantage in the production of "cleaner" goods and services.

Delaying environmental efforts risks masking competitiveness losses of dirty sectors

Halting environmental efforts risks artificially preserving the competitiveness of "dirty" sectors. Tightening environmental policies often faces resistance from sectors which fear losing their competitiveness, namely the "dirty" industries. Shying away from implementing more stringent environmental policies in the first place, however, only preserves the seemingly competitive "dirty" sectors, reducing incentives for investment in cleaner technologies and decreases any potential first-mover advantages.

Joint global climate commitments should be supplemented with agreements for clean technology transfers

A global climate agreement, which implies a tightening of environmental policies around the world would leave less room for offshoring of carbon-intensive sectors. If the gap in environmental policies across countries decreases due to a global effort of strengthening environmental policies, domestic "dirty" sectors are less likely to move to another country with laxer environmental policy standards. Additional agreements for clean technology transfers across countries might further help to ensure a global level-playing field of environmental policies.

Notes

[1] This chapter is a summary of the paper "Do Environmental Policies affect Global Value Chains? A New Perspective on the Pollution Haven Hypothesis" by T. Koźluk and C. Timiliotis (2016), published as OECD Economics Department Working Paper, No. 1282.

References

Albrizio, S., T. Koźluk and V. Zipperer (2017), "Environmental policies and productivity growth: Evidence across industries and firms", *Journal of Environmental Econonics and Management*, Vol. 81, pp. 209-226. [18]

Baldwin, J. and Yan (2014), "Les chaines de valeur mondiales et la productivité des entreprises manufacturières au Canada", *Série de documents de recherche sur l'analyse économique (AE), Statistics Canada, Direction des études analytiques*. [1]

Barro, R. and J. Lee (2010), "A New Data Set of Education Attainment in the World, 1950-2010", *NBER Working Paper*, Vol. 15902, http://dx.doi.org/DOI 10.3386/w15902. [22]

De Sousa, J. (2012), "The currency union effect on trade is decreasing over time", *Economic Letters*, Vol. 117/3, pp. 917-920, https://doi.org/10.1016/j.econlet.2012.07.009. [20]

Ederington, J., A. Levinson and J. Minier (2005), "Footlose and pollution-free", *The Review of Economics and Statistics*, Vol. 87/1, pp. 92-99, https://www.mitpressjournals.org/doi/pdf/10.1162/0034653053327658. [8]

Frankel, J. (1997), *Regional Trading Blocs in the World Trading System*, https://www.piie.com/publications/chapters_preview/72/1iie2024.pdf. [10]

Frankel, J. and A. Rose (2002), "An estimate of the effect of common currencies on trade and income", *The Quarterly Journal of Economics*, Vol. 117/2, pp. 437-466, https://www.jstor.org/stable/2696432. [11]

Johansson, Å. et al. (2014), "What Explains the Volume and Composition of Trade?: Industrial Evidence from a Panel of Countries", *OECD Economics Department Working Papers*, No. 1128, OECD Publishing, Paris, https://dx.doi.org/10.1787/5jz2hz3tm6vj-en. [17]

Kellenberg, D. (2009), "An empirical investigation of the pollution haven effect with strategic environment and trade policy", *Journal of International Economics*, Vol. 78, pp. 242-255, https://doi.org/10.1016/j.jinteco.2009.04.004. [6]

Kowalski, P. (2011), "Comparative Advantage and Trade Performance: Policy Implications", *OECD Trade Policy Papers*, No. 121, OECD Publishing, Paris, https://dx.doi.org/10.1787/5kg3vwb8g0hl-en. [21]

Koźluk, T. and C. Timiliotis (2016), "Do Environmental Policies affect Global Value Chains? A new perspective on the pollution haven hypothesis", *Economics Department Working Papers*, No. ECO/WKP(2016)6, OECD, Paris. [2]

Manova, K. (2013), "Credit constraints, heterogeneous firms and international trade", *The Review of Economic Studies*, Vol. 80, pp. 711-744, https://doi.org/10.1093/restud/rds036. [13]

McCallum, J. (1995), "National border matter: Canada-U.S. regional trade patterns", *American Economic Review*, Vol. 85/6, pp. 615-623, https://www.jstor.org/stable/pdf/2118191.pdf. [9]

McGuire, M. (1982), "Regulation, factor rewards, and international trade", *Journal of Public Economics*, Vol. 17/3, https://www.sciencedirect.com/science/article/pii/004727278290069X (accessed on 17 January 2019). [3]

Miroudot, S., R. Lanz and A. Ragoussis (2009), "Trade in Intermediate Goods and Services", *OECD Trade Policy Working Paper, No. 93*, https://doi.org/10.1787/5kmlcxtdlk8r-en. [19]

Nicoletti, G. et al. (2003), "Policies and International Integration: Influences on Trade and Foreign Direct Investment", *OECD Economics Department Working Papers*, No. 359, OECD Publishing, Paris, https://dx.doi.org/10.1787/062321126487. [14]

Nuun, N. (2007), "Relationship-specificity, incomplete contracts, and the pattern of trade", *Quarterly Journal of Economics*, Vol. CXXII, pp. 569-600, https://scholar.harvard.edu/files/nunn/files/contracts_trade_qje.pdf. [12]

Porter, M. (1991), "America's green strategy", *Scientific American*, https://books.google.fr/books?hl=fr&lr=&id=i7UDHIOGfPEC&oi=fnd&pg=PA33&dq=porter+americas+green+strategy&ots=AN4z5Eq9YG&sig=GXJp7n_hiAcLtkpn-sCpUDK1UzU (accessed on 17 January 2019). [4]

Porter, M. and C. van der Linde (1995), "Toward a New Conception of the Environment-Competitiveness Relationship", *Journal of Economic Perspectives*, Vol. 9/4, pp. 97-118, http://dx.doi.org/10.1257/jep.9.4.97. [5]

Rajan, R. and L. Zingales (1998), "Financial Dependence and Growth", *The American Economic Review*, Vol. 88/3, pp. 559-586, https://www.jstor.org/stable/116849?seq=1#metadata_info_tab_contents. [16]

Sato, M. et al. (2019), "International and sectoral variation in industry energy prices 1995-2015", *Energy Economics*, Vol. 78, pp. 235-258. [23]

Van Beers, C. and J. van den Bergh (1997), "An empirical multi-country analysis of the impact of environmental regulations on foreign trade flows", *Kyklos*, Vol. 50, pp. 29-46, https://doi.org/10.1111/1467-6435.00002. [7]

Yi, K. (2003), "Can vertical specialization explain the growth of world trade?", *The Journal of Political Economy*, Vol. 111/1, pp. 52-102, https://www.jstor.org/stable/10.1086/344805. [15]

7 The European Union Emissions Trading System and its economic and environmental impacts

The European Union Emissions Trading System (EU ETS) is currently the largest emissions trading system globally in terms of greenhouse gases covered. With an increasing number of emissions trading systems being implemented around the world, it is important to understand the environmental and economic impacts such a system might have. This chapter[1] provides a causal analysis of the impact of the introduction of the EU ETS on regulated companies. To evaluate the impact on carbon emissions, installation-level data on CO_2 emissions is used for four European countries, while the analysis focuses on the economic impacts on firms' revenues, assets, profits and employment, it uses firm-level data for 31 European countries. The empirical analysis uses a matching methodology combined with a difference-in-differences estimation to provide a causal estimate of the policy's impact. The analysis finds that the introduction of the EU ETS led to a reduction of carbon emissions by 10% between 2005 and 2012. The impact on economic outcomes is either insignificant or positive, suggesting that the potential fears in terms of competitiveness loss of the European industry have been exaggerated.

Background

The largest emissions trading system in the world

The European Union Emissions Trading System (EU ETS) was introduced in 2005 and is the largest emissions trading system in the world in terms of greenhouse gases covered. The cap-and-trade mechanism covers around 12 000 energy-intensive installations in 31 countries, accounting for 40% of the European Union's total greenhouse gas emissions. Around 8 000 companies owning these installations are thus incentivised to reduce their carbon emissions. The trading of emission allowance certificates ensures that emission reductions are achieved in a cost-effective manner. Nonetheless, concerns that carbon pricing might hamper the competitiveness of the European industry have been present since the introduction of the scheme.

Emissions cap and verified emissions decreased over time

The EU ETS was set up with a steadily declining overall emissions cap. Being one of the first carbon emissions trading schemes, the EU ETS has been divided into different trading phases in order to be able to implement adjustments if necessary. The first trading phase, from 2005 to 2007 was a pilot which prohibited banking and borrowing of allowances across trading phases. The second (2008-12) and third (2013-20) trading phases allowed firms to bank unused allowances for later use. Figure 7.1. shows the emission cap as well as the verified emissions for the three trading phases. While it can be seen from the figure that overall verified emissions declined over time, it is a priori not clear whether this is a causal effect of the EU ETS or whether this development is due to other factors like technological progress or macroeconomic developments such as business cycle fluctuations or structural changes of the European economy.

Figure 7.1. Overall cap and verified emissions from EU ETS installations (2005 – 2015)

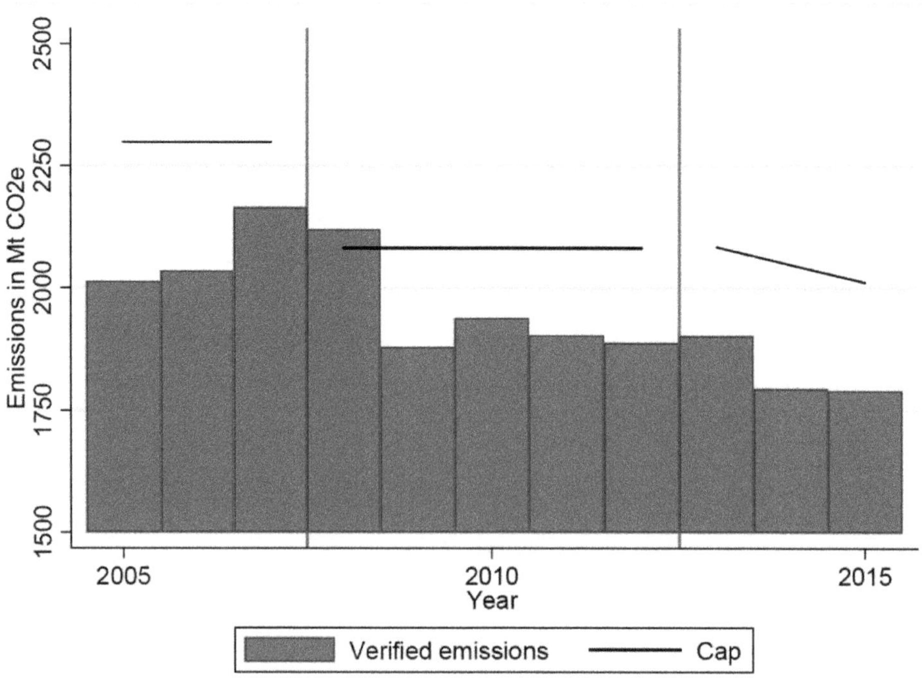

Note: Calculations by Dechezleprêtre, Nachtigall and Venmans (2018[1]), based on data from the European Transaction Log (EUTL).

Pollution Haven and Porter Hypothesis – the theory is ambiguous

As discussed in previous chapters, environmental policy tools, especially market-based ones, impose additional costs on companies which might divert resources away from productive activities. Two well-known hypotheses describe the potential effect of environmental regulation on productivity and hence competitiveness. First, the Pollution Haven Hypothesis predicts that parts of the regulated industry will either move abroad or close down because of foreign competition (Levinson and Taylor, 2008[2]), creating carbon leakage, especially when environmental policy stringency is weaker outside the ETS. Second, the Porter Hypothesis suggests that productivity and thus competitiveness of the regulated industry might increase in response to tighter environmental policy, as the latter induces innovation that would not have happened in the absence of the policy (Porter, 1991[3]; Porter and van der Linde, 1995[4]).

Empirical studies on the EU ETS focused on either economic or environmental outcomes so far

There is only a nascent field of literature investigating the environmental and economic outcomes of environmental policies at the same time. While there is a number of studies investigating either the environmental or the economic effects of the EU ETS, combined analyses of economic and environmental outcomes are scarce. Studies only looking at the environmental outcomes of the EU ETS find reductions of CO_2 emissions attributable to the EU ETS, with abatement rates ranging between 2.4% and 4.7% (see Martin, Muûls and Wagner (2016[5]) for a literature overview). Abatement rates are, however, found to vary significantly across sectors. Studies focusing only on the economic effects of the EU ETS (see Martin, Muûls and Wagner (2016[5]) for a review) found positive effects on value added, turnover and investment (Marin, Marino and Pellegrin, 2018[6]), no or slightly positive effects on employment (Anger and Oberndorfer, 2008[91]; Marin, Marino and Pellegrin, 2018[142]; Commins et al., 2011[92]; with the exception of Abrell, Ndoye Faye and Zachmann (2011[7]) who find a slight decrease in employment), and either positive (Commins et al., 2011[8]; Löschel, Lutz and Managi, 2016[9]; Calligaris, D'Arcangelo and Pavan, 2018[10]) or negative (Marin, Marino and Pellegrin, 2018[6]) effects on total factor productivity growth. One of the most comprehensive studies in terms of the countries covered provides evidence that the EU ETS has increased innovation activity in low-carbon technologies among regulated companies by 30% compared to a scenario where the EU ETS would not have been in place (Calel and Dechezleprêtre, 2016[11]). Regarding the evaluation of the joint EU ETS effects on carbon emissions and firm performance, four studies – each looking at one particular country – have been carried out so far. One study looking at France shows that the EU ETS reduced carbon emissions of regulated plants by 13%, but finds no statistically significant changes to employment, value added or the capital stock, suggesting that the effects of the ETS on the competitiveness of regulated firms has been limited (Wagner et al., 2018[12]). Another study focusing on Germany finds that the EU ETS reduced carbon emissions of regulated firms by 25%, while no significant impact on employment was found (Petrick and Wagner, 2014[13]). A study on Norway finds that emissions were reduced by 30% in the second trading phase of the EU ETS and that value-added and labour productivity of firms increased significantly (Klemetsen, Rosendahl and Jakobsen, 2020[14]), potentially because of the free allocation of allowance certificates. Looking at the initial phase of the EU ETS, a study on Lithuania finds no significant impact on carbon emissions or on firms' profitability (Jaraite and Di Maria, 2016[15]).

Contribution of this study – first comprehensive study of environmental and economic effects of the EU ETS

This study provides the first comprehensive study of the joint environmental and economic effects of the EU ETS. The study evaluates the first ten years of the EU ETS, from 2005 to 2015 (2005-12 for carbon emissions) and provides the first European-wide analysis of the effects on carbon emissions as well as on firm performance, as measured by revenues, assets, profits and employment. Using matching techniques and a difference-in-difference estimation allows for the causal estimation of the EU ETS effects.

Empirical set-up

Causal analysis using a difference-in-difference approach

The empirical analysis relies on a quasi-experimental setting where the identification of the causal effect exploits sector-specific capacity thresholds that determine inclusion in the EU ETS. The EU ETS only covers installations above a certain threshold of production capacity while installations below this threshold are not regulated. In order to evaluate the impact of being regulated under the EU ETS, the analysis can thus compare installations above the threshold with similar installations just below the threshold. Similarly, firms owning at least one installation above the threshold might be very close (in terms of turnover, number of employees, and so on) to unregulated firms owning only installations below the threshold. It is thus possible to compare regulated firms with unregulated firms, located in the same country, operating in the same sector and having similar characteristics, and use this set of firms as a control group. The regulated and unregulated entities are matched based on characteristics in the years before the introduction of the EU ETS. The matching is then combined with a difference-in-difference estimation, which compares regulated and unregulated entities before and after the introduction of the EU ETS. This approach allows to control for confounding factors which affect both regulated and unregulated installations as well as for unobserved heterogeneity.

Empirical model

The difference-in-difference model is estimated at the installation or firm level, depending on the outcome investigated, and is based on the following equation:

$$Y_{it} = \alpha ETS_i + \beta post + \gamma ETS_i post + \delta_i + \theta_t + \varepsilon_{it}$$

where Y_{it} is either carbon emissions of installation *i*, or turnover, assets, number of employees, profit or return on assets of firm *i* at time *t*. ETS_i is a dummy variable indicating whether the installation/firm was regulated by the EU ETS or not, $post$ is a dummy variable indicating the post-treatment period (after 2005), and $ETS_i post$ is the interaction term between the two variables. δ_i are installation/firm fixed effects, θ_t are year fixed effects. ε_{it} reflects the remaining error term. Depending on the specification and the nature of the dependent variable, an OLS or a Poisson estimator is used.

Data

The data on carbon emissions are taken from the national Pollution Release and Transfer Registers (PRTRs) and cover France, the Netherlands, Norway and the United Kingdom as the threshold for reporting emissions in the pollution release registries of these countries is comparably low (below 10 kt per year) and therefore provides emission information on many installations which are not covered by the EU ETS. The European Union Transaction Log (EUTL) is used to identify installations covered by the EU ETS. Matching the regulated installations to unregulated ones yields a final sample of 408 installations for the analysis of the environmental outcome. Regarding the analysis of economic outcomes, the dataset covers 31 European countries over the time period 2003 to 2015. The EUTL is used to identify firms owning at least one installation covered by the EU ETS. These firms are considered as regulated by the EU ETS. Data on economic outcomes come from the firm-level database ORBIS. The matched sample size for the analysis of the economic effects covers 3 067 firms.

Results

The EU ETS led to emission reductions, while firm performance was largely unaffected

The empirical results show an average reduction of carbon emissions by 10% in the first two trading phases from 2005 until 2012 (Table 7.1. , column 1). During the first trading phase, carbon emissions were reduced by 6% while in the second trading phase, emissions were reduced by 15%. Figure 7.2. shows the estimated yearly treatment effects of the EU ETS on firms' emissions, indicating that most of the emission reductions took place towards the end of the second trading phase. Regarding firm performance, the analysis shows that the EU ETS led to an increase in revenues by 7% to 18% (depending on the specification and matching algorithm used) and to an increase in fixed assets by (6% to 10%) for regulated firms (Table 7.1. , columns 3 and 4). No statistically significant impact on the number of employees or on profits is found.

Table 7.1. Effects of the EU ETS - main estimation results

Dependent variable:	Carbon emissions	Revenue (log)	Assets (log)	Employees	Profit	ROA
Estimator	OLS	OLS	OLS	Poisson	OLS	OLS
Treatment effect	-0.10*	0.1671***	0.0811***	0.0234	283.6478	0.0002
	(0.06)	(0.0256)	(0.0225)	(0.0214)	(211.2466)	(0.0049)
Installation fixed effect	Yes	No	No	No	No	No
Firm fixed effect	No	Yes	Yes	Yes	Yes	Yes
Sector fixed effect	No	Yes	Yes	Yes	Yes	Yes
Country fixed effect	No	No	No	No	No	No
Year fixed effect	No	No	No	No	No	No
Observations	3 153	42 742	42 640	40 117	42 834	41 666

Notes: Robust standard errors for estimation 1 in parentheses. Clustered standard errors for estimation 2 to 6. ***, ** and * represent p<0.01, p<0.05, p<0.1 respectively.

Figure 7.2. Treatment effect in terms of carbon emissions by year

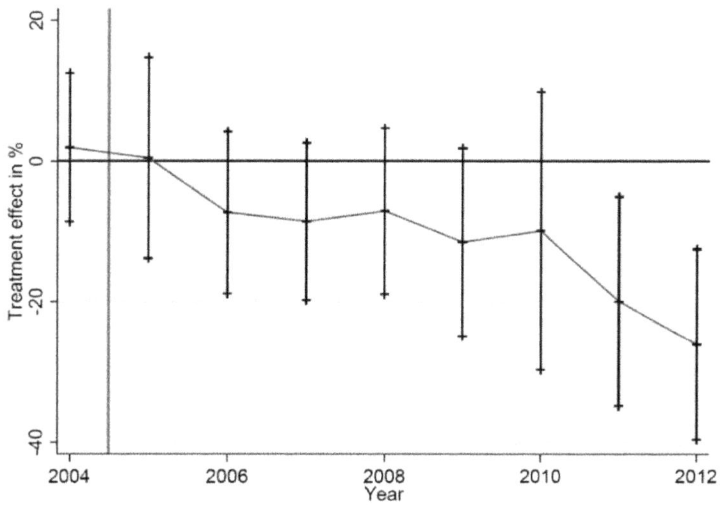

Notes: Point estimates are shown with confidence interval.
Source: Dechezleprêtre, Nachtigall and Venmans (2018[1]).

The effects of the EU ETS are heterogeneous across sectors and vary with the number of free allowances granted

The impact of the EU ETS on emission reductions vary across installation size, sector and the level of free allowance allocation (see Dechezleprêtre, Nachtigall and Venmans (2018[1]) for detailed estimation results). Emission reductions were strongest for larger installations. Large firms may be more responsive to carbon pricing because pollution control technologies are typically capital intensive and involve a high fixed cost. Larger firms may be able to spread fixed costs over higher output, lowering the cost per unit of production. The effect is found to differ across sector, with the chemicals, non-metallic mineral products and electricity sectors showing the largest reductions in carbon emissions. The results also show that reductions in emissions are lower for installations, which were granted more free allowances. Installations with an over-allocation of free allowances[2] did not reduce their emissions significantly.

Turning to the economic impacts, the positive and statistically significant effect on revenue and assets is present in all three phases of the EU ETS, even though the impact is larger in phase 2 and 3. The effect is slightly larger for smaller firms. Looking at individual sectors, the paper shows that no single sector was negatively hit by the EU ETS in terms of firm performance. The positive effect seems, however, to be driven by the minerals, metals, electricity and heat sectors. The electricity and heat sector did not only increase revenue and assets but also employment and return on assets – probably a consequence of effective cost pass-through combined with free allowance allocation.

Robustness checks

The results are robust to several robustness checks, such as excluding the largest installations, excluding outliers and using a balanced sample. In order to address the concern that the matched sample of installations is rather small and thus an extrapolation of the results to other EU-countries might be questionable, the matching procedure is relaxed, which results in almost doubling the sample size. The point estimate of the treatment effect is reduced in the larger sample but remains statistically significant. Overall, the different specifications yield a range of estimated effects of the EU ETS on carbon emissions in the range of a reduction of 6% to 12%.

Conclusion

The EU ETS led to emission reductions of regulated firms, but did not negatively affect their economic performance

The analysis of this study shows that the introduction of the EU ETS led to a reduction in carbon emissions of around 10% between 2005 and 2012. Most of this reduction took place in the second trading period, where carbon emissions were reduced by 15%. The effect is found to be strongest for larger installations, and is more prevalent in the chemicals, non-metallic mineral products and electricity sectors. Free allocation of allowances is associated with a smaller emission reduction, with over-allocated installations not reducing their emissions at all. Regarding economic outcomes, the study did not find statistically significant effects on employment or profits, but a positive effect on revenues and fixed assets of regulated firms. One explanation could be that the EU ETS induced investment in low-carbon technologies, which increased output per worker, but more research is needed to understand the drivers of these effects.

A larger database would strengthen the external validity of the results

While the analysis of the impact on economic outcomes covers all countries included in the EU ETS, this is not the case for the analysis of carbon emissions. This part of the analysis is based on a small sample of installations, which makes an extrapolation of these results to all EU ETS-regulated firms not suitable.

Increasing the size of the underlying database would certainly strengthen the external validity of the study. However, the study does provide a first step towards a geographically comprehensive analysis of the EU ETS.

Higher carbon prices would likely reduce emissions further, but might lead to different economic impacts on firms

While the EU ETS led to emission reductions, this was not accompanied by negative economic impacts on regulated firms. This could justify tighter environmental policies, which means in this case, higher carbon prices in the EU ETS. Increasing the price of allowances, for example, by further restricting the number of free allowances distributed, would therefore likely increase emissions reductions. Indeed, the study suggests that, had the regulated installations only received half of their free allowances, the reduction in carbon emissions induced by the EU ETS would have been around 25% instead of the estimated 10% (see Dechezleprêtre, Nachtigall and Venmans (2018[1]) for a detailed calculation). However, it is important to keep in mind that the results on economic impacts are valid for a period where carbon prices were relatively low, at around EUR 10/tonne of CO_2. The impact on firm performance might well differ in a context of much higher carbon prices.

Notes

[1] This chapter is a summary of the paper "The joint impact of the European Union emissions trading system on carbon emissions and economic performance" by A. Dechezleprêtre, D. Nachtigall and F. Venmans (2018[1]), published as OECD Economics Department Working Paper No. 1515.

[2] The over-allocation of free allowances means that installations received more free allowances than they required to cover their emissions.

References

Abrell, J., A. Ndoye Faye and G. Zachmann (2011), "Assessing the impact of the EU ETS using firm level data", *Bruegel Working Paper*, https://www.bruegel.org/2011/07/assessing-the-impact-of-the-eu-ets-using-firm-level-data/. [7]

Calel, R. and A. Dechezleprêtre (2016), "Environmental Policy and Directed Technological Change: Evidence from the European Carbon Market", *The Review of Economics and Statistics*, Vol. 98/1, pp. 173-191, https://doi.org/10.1162/REST_a_00470. [11]

Calligaris, S., F. D'Arcangelo and G. Pavan (2018), *The Impact of the European Carbon Market on Firm Productivity: Evidence from Italian Manufacturing Firms*, https://www.tse-fr.eu/publications/impact-european-carbon-market-firm-productivity-evidence-italian-manufacturing-firms. [10]

Commins, N. et al. (2011), "Climate Policy & Corporate Behavior", *Energy Journal*, Vol. 32/4, pp. 51-68, https://www.jstor.org/stable/41323333. [8]

Dechezleprêtre, A., D. Nachtigall and F. Venmans (2018), "The joint impact of the European Union emissions trading system on carbon emissions and economic performance", *OECD Economics Department Working Papers*, No. 1515, OECD Publishing, Paris, https://dx.doi.org/10.1787/4819b016-en. [1]

Jaraite, J. and C. Di Maria (2016), "Did the EU ETS make a difference? An empirical assessment using Lithuanian firm-level data", *The Energy Journal*, Vol. 37/1, pp. 1-23, http://dx.doi.org/doi: 10.5547/01956574.37.2.jjar. [15]

Klemetsen, M., K. Rosendahl and A. Jakobsen (2020), "The impacts of the EU ETS on Norwegian Plants' Environmental and Economic Performance", *Climate Change Economics*, Vol. 11/1, https://doi.org/10.1142/S2010007820500062. [14]

Levinson, A. and M. Taylor (2008), "Unmasking the pollution haven effect", *International Economic Review*, Vol. 49/1, pp. 223-254, http://dx.doi.org/10.1111/j.1468-2354.2008.00478.x. [2]

Löschel, A., B. Lutz and S. Managi (2016), "The Impacts of the EU ETS on Efficiency - An Empirical Analysis for German Manufacturing Firms", *ZEW Discussion Papers*, Vol. 16-089, https://doi.org/10.1016/j.reseneeco.2018.03.001. [9]

Marin, G., M. Marino and C. Pellegrin (2018), "The impact of the European Union Emission Trading Scheme on Multiple Measures of Economic Performance", *Environmental and Resource Economics*, Vol. 71/2, pp. 551-582, http://dx.doi.org/doi: 10.1007/s10640-017-0173-0. [6]

Martin, R., M. Muûls and U. Wagner (2016), "The impact of the European Union Emissions Trading Scheme on regulated firms: what is the evidence after ten years?", *Review of Environmental Economics and Policy*, Vol. 10/1, pp. 129-148, https://doi.org/10.1093/reep/rev016. [5]

Petrick, S. and U. Wagner (2014), "The impact of carbon trading on industry: Evidence from German manufacturing (RMS)", *Kiel Working Paper*, Vol. No. 1912, https://www.econstor.eu/handle/10419/94357. [13]

Porter, M. (1991), "America's green strategy", *Scientific American*, https://books.google.fr/books?hl=fr&lr=&id=i7UDHIOGfPEC&oi=fnd&pg=PA33&dq=porter+americas+green+strategy&ots=AN4z5Eq9YG&sig=GXJp7n_hiAcLtkpn-sCpUDK1UzU (accessed on 17 January 2019). [3]

Porter, M. and C. van der Linde (1995), "Toward a New Conception of the Environment-Competitiveness Relationship", *Journal of Economic Perspectives*, Vol. 9/4, pp. 97-118, http://dx.doi.org/10.1257/jep.9.4.97. [4]

Wagner, U. et al. (2018), *Emissions Trading, Firm Behavior, and the Environment: Evidence from French Manufacturing Firms*, http://conference.iza.org/conference_files/EnvEmpl2014/martin_r7617.pdf. [12]

8 The joint effects of energy prices and carbon taxes in the French manufacturing sector

This chapter focuses on the environmental and economic effects of energy prices and carbon taxes in the French manufacturing sector.[1] Like the previous chapter, it analyses the economic effects of environmental policies alongside environmental ones, focusing here on the effect of energy taxes. These taxes are a main policy instrument to reduce energy consumption and associated carbon emissions. France is one of several OECD countries that have introduced a carbon tax, which translated into higher energy prices. The study uses a unique micro-level dataset and an instrumental variable approach to evaluate the joint effects of changes in energy prices on the French manufacturing sector. The firm-level analysis shows that a 10% increase in energy prices results in a reduction of energy use by 6%, of carbon emissions by 9% and of employment on average by 2%. However, the effect on employment differs according to the size and energy-intensity of the firm. Small and medium-sized enterprises, which stay in business after the energy price increase do not decrease their workforce. The industry-level analysis shows that there is no change in the number of jobs at the sector-level, implying that jobs are not lost but reallocated. The reason for this absence of an effect at the sector level is two opposing factors: large and energy-intensive firms reduce employment in the short run, while smaller energy-efficient firms increase employment in response to output reallocation.

Background

Energy taxes are a commonly used policy instrument to reduce energy use and thus carbon emissions

Among market-based environmental policy instruments, energy taxes are a common tool to incentivise reductions in energy use and thus ultimately in carbon emissions (Jacobsen, 2015[1]). While these market-based instruments are associated with lower abatement costs compared to regulatory instruments (Holland, 2012[2]) and do not interfere with consumption choices (Gayer and Viscusi, 2013[3]), they do impose real costs on consumers. Because energy taxation increases production costs, policy makers fear negative consequences for firms in terms of a reduction of output or employment from these policies.

The design of the French carbon tax

In 2013, France introduced a carbon tax. After a gradual phase-in, the carbon tax amounted to EUR 44.6 per tonne of carbon since 2019 (Figure 8.1.). Evaluating the environmental and economic impacts of this large-scale policy instrument is crucial to understand actual firm-level responses to this policy.

Figure 8.1. Evolution of French carbon tax over time (2013-19)

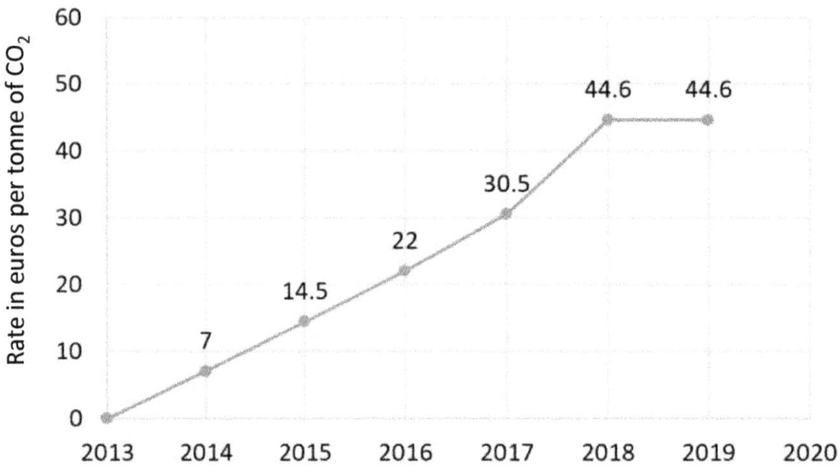

Note: The data are based on various French laws (article 266 quinquies B of the French customs law, the 2018 Finance Bill, and the 2019 Finance Bill).
Source: Dussaux (2020[4]).

Firms might react differently to changes in energy prices depending on their size

There are several reasons why firms' reactions to changes in energy prices are likely to differ according to the firm's size. First, large firms are more efficient than small firms not only because of economies of scale but also because they can incur the fixed cost required for energy efficiency investments. Therefore, smaller firms have more room for energy-efficiency gains than larger firms, which might not be able to reduce energy use without cutting output and thus lowering employment. Similarly, larger firms might have greater capacity to offshore or outsource part of their production in response to changes in energy prices, while small and medium-sized firms might be driven out of the market. This could imply that large firms are more affected by higher energy prices in terms of employment or output. Last but not least, small surviving firms might be able to capture the market share of other small firms that exit the market because of the energy cost increase. However, whether and by how much the effects may differ according to the size of firms remains an empirical question.

The empirical literature has so far ignored heterogeneous effects along energy-intensity and firm size

The study summarised here contributes to the literature investigating the direct effects of higher energy prices on energy use as well as to the literature evaluating joint outcomes of environmental policies more broadly. The previous literature investigating the relationship between energy prices and energy use has found non-negligible fuel and electricity price elasticities, especially in the long run (Houthakker, 1951[5]; Taylor, 1975[6]; Bohi and Zimmerman, 1984[7]; Al-Sahlawi, 1989[8]; Espey, 1996[9]; Brons et al., 2008[10]; Havranek, Irsova and Janda, 2012[11]; Labandeira, Labeaga and Lopez-Otero, 2017[12]).

This study adds to this literature by investigating the way in which firms actually reduce their energy consumption, i.e. through fuel switching, input substitution or investment in pollution abatement technologies. The literature investigating economic and environmental outcomes of changes in environmental policies (Greenstone, List and Syverson, 2012[13]; Walker, 2013[14]; Martin, de Preux and Wagner, 2014[15]; Wagner et al., 2018[16]; Flues and Lutz, 2015[17]; Gerster, 2015[18]; Petrick and Wagner, 2014[19]) finds a reduction in the use of energy inputs and thus in carbon emissions in response to tighter environmental policies, but is ambiguous regarding the effect on economic outcomes.

Firm and sector heterogeneity is often not investigated in detail and the economic outcomes considered vary across studies. The most relevant paper to the study at hand also investigates the impact of energy prices on employment and environmental performance in the French manufacturing sector for the years 1997 to 2010 (Marin and Vona, 2017[20]), but focuses only on surviving plants. Marin and Vona (2017[20]) find that a 10% increase in energy prices is related to a reduction of 6% in energy consumption, an 11% reduction in CO_2 emissions and a decrease in employment by 2.6% with a small impact on wages and productivity. The study by Marin and Vona (2017) is based on plant-level data and does not investigate firm-level responses such as real output, investment and patenting activity.

The combination of a firm-level and an industry-level analysis offers deeper insights into the mechanisms behind the effects

The study summarised in this chapter offers one of the first comprehensive, causal analyses of the effect of energy taxes by combining a firm-level with an industry-level analysis. Using a unique dataset of 8 000 French manufacturing firms from 2001 to 2016, an instrumental variable approach is used to provide a causal analysis. The study investigates multiple economic outcomes, namely output, employment, investment in terms of pollution abatement capital expenditure, and patent applications. In addition, firm-level heterogeneity is explored in terms of the energy-intensity and the size of firms. The industry-level analysis complements the firm-level analysis by taking into account reallocation effects between firms.

Empirical set-up

A causal analysis using an instrumental variable approach

The empirical analysis comprises two parts, a firm-level and an industry-level analysis. The firm-level analysis identifies firms' responses to exogenous changes in energy prices by relying on the use of the fixed-weight energy price index by Sato et al. (2019[21]) as an instrumental variable for average energy costs. Using fixed instead of average weights helps to avoid endogeneity issues associated with firms potentially being able to affect energy demand and energy prices simultaneously. Moreover, these energy prices are measured at the industry-level and can therefore be assumed to be exogenous at the firm-level.

This is not the case at the industry-level, making this analysis rely on stronger assumptions than the firm-level analysis. The strong advantage of the industry-level analysis is, however, that it is able to analyse between-firm adjustments, for example, through new firms entering the market as it is not restricted to surviving firms. The comprehensive employment data covers the whole population of French firms, thus allowing to calculate job destruction and job creation metrics, following Davis and Haltiwanger (1992[22]).

Empirical model

The following model is estimated at the firm-level for several outcome variables, using a fixed-effects, two-stage least squares estimator:

$$y_{it} = \beta_0 + \beta_1 Cost_{it-1} + \beta_2 X_{it-1} + \mu_i + \gamma_t + \varepsilon_{it}$$

where y_{it} is an outcome variable of firm *i* at time *t* (i.e. energy use, number of workers, real output, etc.). $Cost$ is the log of average energy cost measured by the ratio between energy expenditure (electricity and other energy carriers) and the purchased quantity in tonnes of oil equivalent. X is a vector of firm-level control variables, including a dummy equal to 1 when the firm is subject to the European Union Emissions Trading System and the average age of the firm's plant. These control variables are lagged by one year in order to account for the time lag firms need to adjust to new energy prices. μ_i are firm fixed effects, γ_t are year dummies and ε_{it} is the remaining error term. In order to test for heterogeneous effects across firm size, two interaction terms are added to the model, differentiating the effect by firm size and energy intensity. The average energy cost is interacted with (i) a dummy variable equal to 1, if the firm has less than 250 employees in the first year it is observed, and (ii) a continuous variable indicating the energy use per employee of the firm in the first year it is observed.

The empirical model at the industry level differs slightly from the firm-level model, with the following equation being estimated:

$$y_{kt} = \alpha_0 + \beta FEPI_{kt-1} + \lambda_t + \gamma_k + \varepsilon_{kt}$$

where y_{kt} is a job flow metric in industry *k* at time *t* (i.e. job creation rate, job destruction rate, net change in jobs), $FEPI_{kt-1}$ is the lagged fixed-weight energy price index (used as an instrument for average energy cost in the firm-level analysis), λ_t are time fixed effects, γ_k are sector fixed effects, and ε_{kt} is the remaining error term.

Data

The dataset used in this study covers 8 000 firms in the French manufacturing sector over the period 2001 to 2016. The dataset combines several databases which are managed by the French Statistical Office (INSEE): Data on energy consumption and expenditure comes from the EACEI (Enquête Annuelle sur les Consommations d'Énergie dans l'Industrie) survey, financial data from FARE (Fichier approché des résultats d'Esane) and FICUS (Fichier de comptabilité unifié dans SUSE), patent data from the PATSTAT database maintained by the European Patent Office, and pollution abatement investment data from the Antipol survey. The emission data are calculated based on the energy consumption from the EACEI survey and CO_2 emission factors from the French Environment and Energy Management Agency (ADEME). As these data are available at the plant level but the data on economic outcomes are available at the firm level, the emission data are aggregated at the firm level, ensuring that only observations are used where all plants belonging to a firm are available in the data. The dataset used for the analysis on investment, built from the Antipol survey, is smaller than the firm-level dataset for the other economic outcomes.

Results

The French carbon tax led to CO_2 reductions at the firm level

The results of the study show an average reduction of energy and fossil fuel use, as well as a reduction in CO_2 emissions and workers in response to higher energy prices (Table 8.1). A 10% increase in energy costs leads to a decrease of 5.9% in energy use and a reduction of fossil fuel use of 6.5%. The reduction in CO_2 emissions is estimated to be 9.2% and the number of workers declines by 2.2%.

In addition, no statistically significant effect is found for real output and investment. Investigating the channels through which firms react to changing energy prices shows that the energy-intensity is reduced by 5.2% in response to an increase of energy prices by 10%. There is also some statistical evidence that labour, material and capital decrease significantly less than energy use when energy prices rise, suggesting that firms reduce their energy-intensity by substituting energy by other inputs (for detailed results see Dussaux (2020[4])). The reduction in the CO_2 intensity is found to come from substituting fossil fuel use by electricity use.

It is important to note that these reductions estimated at the firm level correspond to a situation where only the energy price of the firm varies. In reality, when the price of a fuel increases in responses to an energy tax, all firms experience a change in their relative energy cost. Energy-intensive firms experience larger energy cost increases than energy-efficient firms. This relative change can lead to market share reallocations between firms. Therefore, it is not possible to extrapolate the effect of a change in the energy price at the aggregate manufacturing level simply by multiplying the estimated effect by the number of firms in a given sector. Consequently, the study also includes an analysis at the industry level that incorporates between-firm reallocations.

Table 8.1. The effect of energy prices on environmental and economic performance - main estimation results

	Environmental performance				Economic performance		
Dependent variable:	Energy use	Electricity use	Fossil fuel use	CO_2 emissions	Workers	Real output	Investment
Energy cost (ln)	-0.592***	-0.144	-0.649***	-0.920***	-0.223***	-0.077	-0.365
	(0.111)	(0.107)	(0.170)	(0.143)	(0.065)	(0.074)	(0.258)
Firm age in years	-0.030***	-0.038***	-0.014	-0.023***	-0.032***	-0.033***	0.004
	(0.007)	(0.007)	(0.009)	(0.007)	(0.004)	(0.004)	(0.012)
ETS dummy	0.019	-0.038	0.081	0.063	0.061**	0.075***	0.032
	(0.037)	(0.036)	(0.061)	(0.043)	(0.026)	(0.029)	(0.074)
Firm fixed effects	Yes	Yes	Yes	Yes	Yes	Yes	Yes
Industry x Year dummies	Yes	Yes	Yes	Yes	Yes	Yes	Yes
Observations	45 903	45 893	40 788	45 903	45 903	45 903	36 327
Number of firms	8 002	7 999	7 048	8 002	8 002	8002	7 168
KP LM statistic	388	388	334	388	388	388	304

Notes: Robust standard errors clustered at the firm level in parentheses. ***, ** and * represent $p<0.01$, $p<0.05$, $p<0.1$ respectively. All outcome variables are logged. All columns are estimated with the TSLS estimator. Energy cost equals the log of the ratio between energy expenditure and energy use. The instrumental variable for average energy cost is the Fixed weight Energy Price Index (FEPI). The Kleibergen-Paap LM (KP LM) statistic is a version of the first-stage F-statistic that is robust to heteroscedasticity.

Effects differ according to firm size, their energy-intensity and the sector they operate in

Analysing potential heterogeneous effects shows that firm responses to increasing energy prices differ significantly according to their initial size and energy-intensity (see Dussaux (2020[4]), for detailed estimation results). Energy-intensive firms react more negatively to higher energy costs in terms of both environmental and economic performance likely because the same energy cost increase penalises these firms more. Small, medium-sized and large firms react differently in terms of both environmental and economic performance. The larger the firm, the more it improves its environmental performance in response to higher energy cost. In terms of economic outcomes, large firms reduce their output by 2.6%, while medium-sized firms do not change their output. Surprisingly, small firms increase their output by 1.4%. The responses in terms of employment also differ greatly. A 10% increase in energy cost does not affect employment of small firms, but reduces it by 2.6% for medium-sized firms and by 5.5% for large firms. Allowing for heterogeneous effects at the sector level shows that firms do not reduce their CO_2 emissions or the number of employees in every sector (Figure 8.2). There are large differences between industries. 79% of the sectors experience a statistically significant reduction in CO_2, 26% reduce employment, 53% reduce CO_2 emissions but not employment, and no sector reduces employment, but not CO_2 emissions in response to higher energy prices. The largest reduction in CO_2 emissions is found for the beverages, wood products and wearing apparel sectors (Figure 8.2, Panel A). For employment, the largest changes are found in the basic metal, plastic and food products sectors (Figure 8.2, Panel B).

Figure 8.2. Changes in CO_2 emissions and workers for a 10% increase in energy cost by sector

Panel A – Change in CO_2 emissions

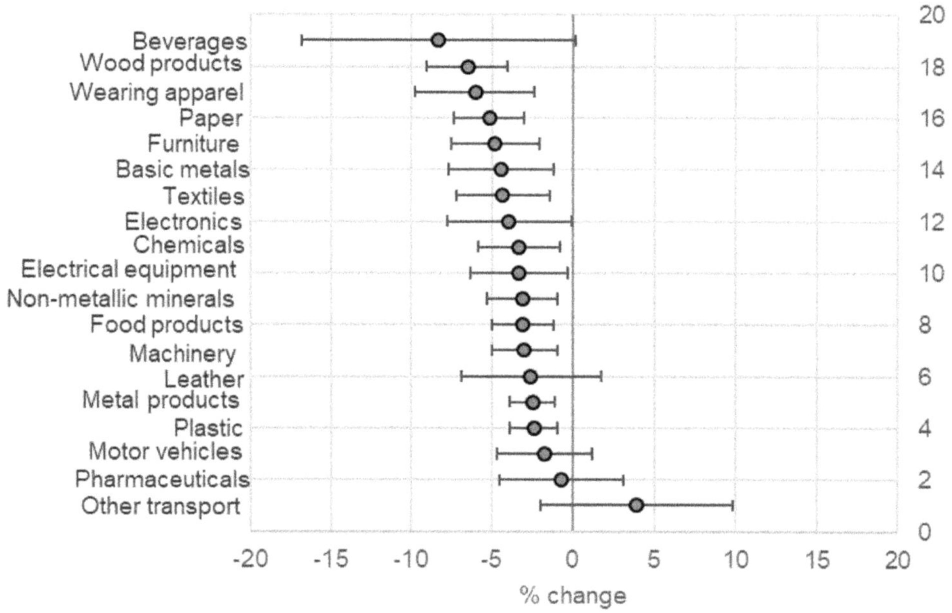

Panel B – Change in the number of workers

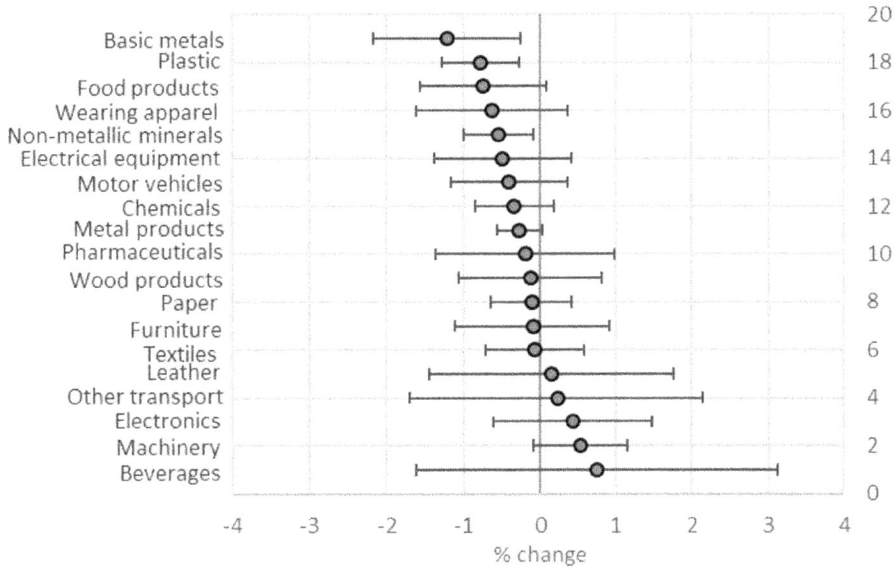

Source: Dussaux (2020).

The industry-level analysis suggests reallocation of workers instead of job losses

The industry-level analysis shows no statistically significant effects of rising energy prices on job destruction, job creation or net employment (see Dussaux (2020[4]), for estimation results). The difference compared to the results from the firm-level analysis is explained by the different sample of firms covered: The firm-level analysis only covers surviving firms while the industry-level accounts for new firms as well as firms exiting the market. An additional analysis of the study finds evidence for the hypothesis that an output reallocation between firms induced by changes in the energy price leads to a reallocation of workers between firms, especially from large energy-intensive firms to energy-efficient SMEs. The negative effect on surviving firms found at the micro level is thus offset by worker reallocation towards energy-efficient firms. This implies that while there is no average effect at the industry level in terms of employment, workers are reallocated within industries and thereby might face adjustment costs.

Robustness checks

The results are robust to many robustness checks, including using different lags of the main explanatory variables and investigating contemporaneous as well as dynamic effects of energy price variation.

Conclusion

The French carbon tax reduced emissions but also triggered a reallocation of workers

The results of the study show that climate policies, which increase energy costs, are effective in terms of carbon emission reductions but also have some small economic effects in terms of employment reallocation. Regarding the environmental effects, the firm-level analysis shows that a 10% increase in energy prices results in a decline in energy use by 6% and a reduction in carbon emissions by 9%. For the economic effects, the study finds that employment can decline for mid-sized and large firms. However, small enterprises, who stay in the market after energy prices rise, do not reduce their employment. The accompanying industry-level analysis shows that at the industry level, the total number of jobs is unaffected. This is due to two opposing effects: On the one hand, employment declines in large and energy-intensive firms and on the other hand, employment rises in energy-efficient firms (including new firms entering the market) as output is reallocated. The overall contribution of changes in energy prices to changes in employment is, however, small: changes in energy prices only triggered the reallocation of 0.25% of total manufacturing employment over the period 2005-16. In comparison, over this period, energy prices rose by 80% and manufacturing employment declined by 26%. In other words, 99% of employment reallocations within the manufacturing sector is due to factors other than changes in the energy price. These effects are, however, heterogeneous across sectors with the beverages, basic metals and wood products sectors having the largest worker reallocation caused by changes in energy prices.

An industry-level analysis of carbon emissions is not possible due to data constraints

The results of the analysis regarding reductions in carbon emissions are only based on the firm-level analysis, implying that the effect is only driven by surviving firms. Due to data limitations, an industry-level analysis of effects of increased energy cost on carbon emissions, similar to the analysis conducted for employment, is not possible. However, a net negative effect at the industry-level in terms of carbon emissions can be expected as the effect on surviving firms in the firm-level analysis is negative and because output reallocation is directed towards more energy-efficient firms in the sectors.

Tighter climate policies reduce carbon emissions, but should be accompanied by complementary labour market policies

Two important policy-relevant conclusions can be drawn from the analysis. First, tighter environmental policies, in the form of higher energy prices, can lead to employment reallocations between firms and industries. While some sectors are affected more than others, complementary labour market policies could help to absorb redistributive implications and reduce the costs for laid-off workers. Second, carbon taxes reduce carbon emissions significantly. As shown in Chapter 1, the carbon tax applied on the French manufacturing sector since 2014, which gradually increased the cost per tonne of CO_2 emission to EUR 45 in 2019 (corresponding to a 5.4% increase in energy prices), decreased carbon emissions by 5% (3.6 Mt of CO_2) with no statistically significant impact on aggregate employment. These two factors imply that there is scope for tighter unilateral environmental policies in order to achieve global climate goals and suggest that accompanying labour market policies could potentially reduce the economic impacts of these policies.

Notes

[1] The chapter is a summary of "The joint effects of energy prices and carbon taxes on environmental and economic performance: Evidence from the French manufacturing sector" (2020[4]) by D. Dussaux, published as OECD Environment Working Paper No. 154.

References

Al-Sahlawi, M. (1989), "The demand for natural gas: a survey of price and income elasticities", *The Energy Journal*, Vol. 10/1, pp. 77-90, https://www.jstor.org/stable/41322309. [8]

Bohi, D. and M. Zimmerman (1984), "An update on econometric studies of energy demand behavior", *Annual Review of Energy*, Vol. 9/1, pp. 105-154, https://doi.org/10.1146/annurev.eg.09.110184.000541. [7]

Brons, M. et al. (2008), "A meta-analysis of the price elasticity of gasoline demand. A SUR approach", *Energy Economics*, Vol. 30/5, pp. 2105-2122, https://doi.org/10.1016/j.eneco.2007.08.004. [10]

Davis, S. and J. Haltiwanger (1992), "Gross job creation, gross job destruction, and employment reallocation", *The Quarterly Journal of Economics*, Vol. 107/3, pp. 819-863, https://www.jstor.org/stable/2118365. [22]

Dussaux, D. (2020), "The joint effects of energy prices and carbon taxes on environmental and economic performance: Evidence from the French manufacturing sector", *OECD Environment Working Papers*, No. 154, OECD Publishing, Paris, https://dx.doi.org/10.1787/b84b1b7d-en. [4]

Espey, M. (1996), "Explaining the variation in elasticity estimates for gasoline demand in the United States: a meta-analysis", *The Energy Journal*, Vol. 17/3, pp. 49-60, https://www.jstor.org/stable/41322693. [9]

Flues, F. and B. Lutz (2015), "Competitiveness Impacts of the German Electricity Tax", *OECD Environment Working Papers*, No. 88, OECD Publishing, Paris, https://dx.doi.org/10.1787/5js0752mkzmv-en. [17]

Gayer, T. and W. Viscusi (2013), "Overriding consumer preferences with energy regulations", *Journal of Regulatory Economics*, Vol. 43/3, pp. 248-264, https://link.springer.com/article/10.1007/s11149-013-9210-2. [3]

Gerster, A. (2015), "Do electricity prices matter: Plant-level evidence from German manufacturing", Vol. Available at SSRN, https://ssrn.com/abstract=2603211. [18]

Greenstone, M., J. List and C. Syverson (2012), "The effects of environmental regulation on the competitiveness of US manufacturing", *NBER Working Paper*, Vol. 18392, http://dx.doi.org/doi: 10.3386/w18392. [13]

Havranek, T., Z. Irsova and K. Janda (2012), "Demand for gasoline is more price-inelastic than commonly thought", *Energy Economics*, Vol. 34/1, pp. 201-207, https://doi.org/10.1016/j.eneco.2011.09.003. [11]

Holland, S. (2012), "Emissions taxes versus intensity standards: Second-best environmental policies with incomplete regulation", *Journal of Environmental Economics and Management*, Vol. 63/3, pp. 375-387, https://doi.org/10.1016/j.jeem.2011.12.002. [2]

Houthakker, H. (1951), "Some calculations on electricity consumption in Great Britain", *Journal of the Royal Statistical Society*, Vol. 114/3, pp. 359-371, https://www.jstor.org/stable/2980781. [5]

Jacobsen, G. (2015), "Do energy prices influence investment in energy efficiency? Evidence from energy star appliances", *Jouranl of Environmental Economics and Management*, Vol. 72, pp. 94-106, https://doi.org/10.1016/j.jeem.2015.09.004. [1]

Labandeira, X., J. Labeaga and X. Lopez-Otero (2017), "A meta-analysis on the price elasticity of energy demand", *Energy Policy*, Vol. 102, pp. 549-568, https://doi.org/10.1016/j.enpol.2017.01.002. [12]

Marin, G. and F. Vona (2017), "The impact of energy prices on employment and environmental performance: Evidence from French manufacturing establishments", *Working Paper 053.2017, Fondazione Eni Enrico Mattei*, https://www.ofce.sciences-po.fr/pdf/dtravail/WP2017-26.pdf. [20]

Martin, R., L. de Preux and U. Wagner (2014), "The impact of a carbon tax on manufacturing: Evidence from microdata", *Journal of Public Economics*, Vol. 117, pp. 1-14, https://doi.org/10.1016/j.jpubeco.2014.04.016. [15]

Petrick, S. and U. Wagner (2014), "The impact of carbon trading on industry: Evidence from German manufacturing (RMS)", *Kiel Working Paper*, Vol. No. 1912, https://www.econstor.eu/handle/10419/94357. [19]

Sato, M. et al. (2019), "International and sectoral variation in industry energy prices 1995-2015", *Energy Economics*, Vol. 78, pp. 235-258. [21]

Taylor, L. (1975), "The demand for electricity: a survey", *The Bell Journal of Economics*, Vol. 6/1, pp. 74-110, https://www.jstor.org/stable/pdf/3003216.pdf. [6]

Wagner, U. et al. (2018), *Emissions Trading, Firm Behavior, and the Environment: Evidence from French Manufacturing Firms*, http://conference.iza.org/conference_files/EnvEmpl2014/martin_r7617.pdf. [16]

Walker, W. (2013), "The transitional costs of sectoral reallocation: evidence from the Clean Air Act and the workforce", *The Quarterly Journal of Economics*, Vol. 1787, https://doi.org/10.1093/qje/qjt022. [14]

9 Impacts of energy prices on economic and environmental performance in the Indonesian manufacturing sector

This chapter focuses on the environmental and economic effects of energy prices in the Indonesian manufacturing sector.[1] In a similar vein to the previous chapter, this chapter evaluates the joint environmental and economic effects of changes in energy prices but this time focusing on an emerging economy. The study uses a rich national dataset, which covers the whole population of medium-sized and large Indonesian manufacturing plants and makes use of geographic, industrial and temporal energy price variations to pursue a causal analysis. The study finds that a 10% increase in energy prices leads to a decline in energy use by 5.2% and to a decline of CO_2 emissions by 5.8%, alongside small, heterogeneous effects on employment. Smaller plants seem to increase their number of workers in response to higher energy prices while larger plants show a slight reduction in employment. Energy price shocks seem to trigger investment in more energy-efficient machinery. Moreover, the probability of plant exit rises particularly for energy-dependent plants in times when energy prices are rising. An additional analysis at the industry-level shows no effects on aggregate net job creation, suggesting that rising energy prices lead to a reallocation of workers but not to permanent employment losses.

Background

Energy costs might increase through energy subsidy reforms

Energy subsidy reforms are a special type of environmental fiscal reform, which aims, for example, at reducing fossil fuel subsidies. These subsidy reforms are, however, often assumed to harm economic growth, especially in emerging economies, because they increase energy costs across all end users. The reaction of firms to energy subsidy reforms depends inter alia on the substitutability of inputs in the production process but also the ability of firms to adapt to changing energy policy environments. Analysing firm reactions to changes in energy prices in general – which reflects the ultimate effect of the reform as previously subsidised firms face higher energy prices – can provide insights into the environmental and economic effects of energy subsidy reforms.

Indonesian energy prices rose, when fuel subsidies were removed

The Indonesian manufacturing sector experienced a steady energy price increase at the same time as fuel subsidies were reduced. As Figure 9.1 shows, energy prices in the Indonesian manufacturing sector rose in the early eighties, followed by a decline in the nineties and a sharp increase since 2000, when fuel subsidies for diesel and marine fuels were removed. In 2005, a presidential decree announced the phasing-out of any remaining fuel subsidies, leading to increased energy prices for industrial users. While Figure 9.1 does not necessarily show a causal relationship, the figure illustrates that Indonesia's fossil fuel subsidy reforms are fairly well reflected by industrial energy prices since 2001.

Figure 9.1. Evolution of Indonesian energy prices and fossil fuel subsidy reform events (1980- 2015)

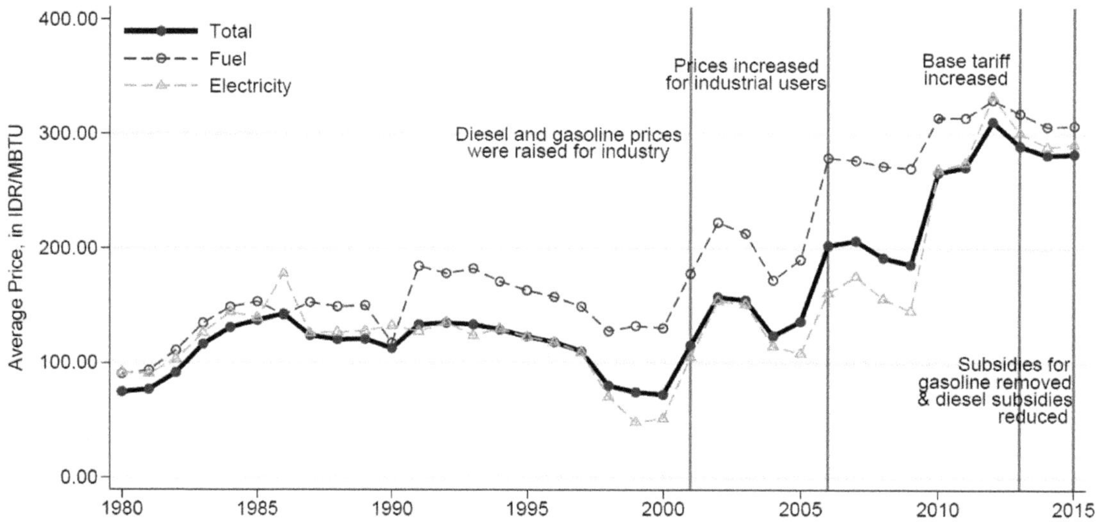

Note: The numbers for the total energy price are based on share-weighted average prices of five major energy sources in the Indonesian manufacturing sector.
Source: Brucal and Dechezleprêtre (2021[1]).

Plants might react in different ways to changes in energy prices

Firms or plants might differ considerably in the way they react to rising energy prices. On the one hand, firms might be able to absorb the price shock and decide not to adjust prices, their output or input in terms of employment. On the other hand, firms might pass through the additional costs or they might change their production processes towards more energy-efficient technologies. Plants might also react differently depending on their size or energy-intensity. Larger plants in energy-intensive sectors (e.g. basic materials producers) might thus improve their energy use more in the event of an energy price shock than smaller plants. Moreover, there is the concern that plants exit the market (Rentschler and Kornejew, 2017[2]) or relocate to other countries (Cole, Elliot and Zhang, 2017[3]), if they are not able to cope with higher energy prices.

The empirical literature has focused on industrial economies so far

The study contributes to the literature investigating the effects of higher energy prices on environmental and economic outcomes. The earlier literature investigating the relationship between energy prices and energy use has found significant effects of fuel and electricity price changes (Houthakker, 1951[4]; Taylor, 1975[5]; Bohi and Zimmerman, 1984[6]; Al-Sahlawi, 1989[7]; Espey, 1996[8]; Brons et al., 2008[9]; Havranek, Irsova and Janda, 2012[10]; Labandeira, Labeaga and Lopez-Otero, 2017[11]). The two most relevant papers for this study have investigated the impact of energy prices on employment and environmental performance in the French manufacturing sector (Dussaux (2020[12]); Marin and Vona, (2017[13])). Both studies find a negative effect of rising energy prices on energy consumption, CO_2 emissions as well as on employment. However, these studies focus on an industrialised economy, leaving the question open whether effects of changing energy prices differ for emerging economies. An analysis of small Indonesian firms (i.e. less than 20 employees) indicates that rising energy prices are associated with a small adverse effect on firm competitiveness, but with increasing energy-efficiency (Rentschler and Kornejew, 2017[2]).

The combination of plant and industry-level analysis provides causal analysis of joint effects for an emerging economy

The study summarised in this chapter offers a causal analysis on the environmental and economic effects of rising energy prices in Indonesia by combining a plant-level with an industry-level analysis. Using a dataset of more than 71 000 Indonesian plants observed over 35 years, from 1980 to 2015, energy price variations at the geographic, industry and temporal dimension are exploited to analyse exogenous changes in energy prices and their implications on plant performance. In addition to environmental outcomes (energy use, CO_2 emissions), the study also investigates the effect on several economic outcomes (e.g. output, employment, capital). The study looks at heterogeneous effects across space and sectors. Moreover, the industry-level analysis sheds light on the employment dynamics following changes in energy prices, providing insights on how whole industries can cope with policy shocks like energy subsidy reforms.

Empirical set-up

The instrumental variable approach based on exogenous price variation allows for causal analysis

The empirical analysis identifies plant responses to exogenous changes in energy prices by using an instrumental variable approach, estimating effects at the plant- as well as at the industry-level. Following Sato et al. (2019[14]), a fixed-weight energy price index is created where the energy price, which an individual plant faces, is calculated by using constant, pre-sample weights of fuel intensity for each plant and province-specific energy prices. The share of each energy source is taken from the first available observation (which is dropped later) and kept constant over the sample period. Using this fixed-weight energy price index as an instrument for average energy costs ensures that effects captured in the analysis are only due to exogenous variations in energy prices and not due to endogenous changes that might be driven by the plant itself. The industry-level analysis allows for investigating between-plant adjustments by going beyond surviving plants in the analysis. In order to analyse employment dynamics at the industry-level, job flow metrics at the province-level are calculated following the method by Davis and Haltiwanger (1992[15]).

Empirical model

The following model is estimated at the plant-level for several outcome variables, using a fixed-effects estimator:

$$\ln(y_{it}) = \beta_0 + \beta_1 \ln(p_{it}) + \mu_i + \gamma_{st} + \delta_{prov-trend} + \epsilon_{it}$$

where y_{it} is an outcome variable of plant *i* at time *t* (i.e. output, energy use, CO_2 emissions). p_{it} is the time-varying energy price index faced by each plant and is calculated by dividing total energy costs by total physical energy use. μ_i are plant-specific, time-invariant fixed effects which control for potentially endogenous plant characteristics, γ_{st} are sector-year fixed effects which control for sudden shocks at the sector level like technological improvements or economic fluctuations, $\delta_{prov-trend}$ are province-specific trends which control for long-term trends in individual regions which might affect energy consumption or sales, and ϵ_{it} is the remaining error term. In order to test for heterogeneous effects of plant size and energy-intensity, two interaction terms are added to the equation: one interaction term between the energy prices and the pre-sample size of the plant (i.e. number of employees) and one interaction term between energy prices and pre-sample energy-intensity.

The empirical model at the industry-level slightly differs from the plant-level model, with the following equation being estimated:

$$y_{pt} = \alpha + \beta p_{pt} + \gamma_t + \lambda_p + \varepsilon_{pt}$$

where y_{pt} is a job flow metric in province *p* at time *t* (i.e. job creation rate, job destruction rate, net change in jobs), p_{pt} is the average plant-specific energy price as used in the plant-level analysis, γ_t are time fixed effects, λ_p are province specific fixed effects, and ε_{pt} is the remaining error term.

Data

The dataset used in this study covers all plants in Indonesia's manufacturing sector, which have 20 or more employees. The data are observed yearly and span from 1980 to 2015. The data are taken from the Indonesian Census of Manufacturing for Medium and Large Enterprises (IBS) conducted by the National Statistical Office and contains detailed information on fuel-specific consumption and electricity use, as well as data on plant performance such as output and employment figures. The fuel and electricity data allow calculating energy use, taking into account own-electricity generation, as well as calculating CO_2 emissions.

Results

Increases in energy prices led to decreasing emissions of Indonesian manufacturing plants

The results of the study show an average reduction of energy use and CO_2 emissions (Table 9.1.). A 10% increase in energy prices leads to a decrease of 5.2% in energy use and a reduction in CO_2 emissions by 5.8%. The analysis of economic outcomes shows that a 10% increase in energy prices leads to a decrease in employment by 0.2%. However, the latter effect is only significant at the 10%-level. No statistically significant effect is found for plant output. Looking at the effect of energy price increases on energy-intensity shows that, for example, a 10% increase in energy prices leads to a reduction in energy (per worker by 5% (Table 9.1. , column 6). This implies that increasing energy prices apparently trigger improvements in the production and/or management processes, ultimately increasing the efficiency of energy use. An additional analysis shows that this efficiency improvement is driven by changes in the capital stock of the plants (see Brucal and Dechezleprêtre (2021[1]) for detailed results).

Table 9.1. Indonesian energy prices - main estimation results

	Environmental performance		Economic performance		Energy intensity
Dependent variable:	Energy use	CO_2 emissions	Output	Employment	Energy per worker
Energy price (log)	-0.523***	-0.577***	0.017	-0.020*	-0.504***
	(0.027)	(0.037)	(0.021)	(0.012)	(0.025)
Plant fixed effects	Yes	Yes	Yes	Yes	Yes
Sector-year fixed effects	Yes	Yes	Yes	Yes	Yes
Province trend	Yes	Yes	Yes	Yes	Yes
Observations	485 621	485 663	485 646	485 672	482 741

Notes: Robust standard errors are clustered at the plant level in parentheses. ***, ** and * represent $p<0.01$, $p<0.05$, $p<0.1$ respectively.

Larger and more energy-intensive plants reduce energy use more than smaller plants

Analysing potential heterogeneous effects shows that changes in energy use depend significantly on the plant's initial output and energy-intensity. Larger plants experience greater reductions in energy use when energy prices increase than smaller plants. In a similar vein, more energy-intensive plants reduce their energy use disproportionately more than energy-efficient plants. Moreover, larger plants also reduce their CO_2-intensity per unit of output more than smaller plants in times of rising energy prices. Relating to the findings in the previous chapter that efficiency improvements are driven by changes in the capital stock, the study also finds that larger plants decrease their capital in response to higher energy prices while smaller plants increase their capital stock. In terms of employment adjustments, smaller plants tend to increase their employment. With increasing plant size, this effect vanishes.

Energy-intensive plants are more likely to be driven out of the market

Looking specifically at plant exit, an additional probit estimation is conducted which analyses the effect of rising energy prices on the probability of market exit (see Brucal and Dechezleprêtre (2021[1]), for details on the estimation and results). The results of this estimation show that increasing energy prices increase the probability of exiting the market, independent of the size of the plant. However, more energy-intensive plants show a higher probability of exit when energy prices rise. Combining these findings with the findings on employment adjustments, this might imply that inefficient plants are exiting the market, leaving more market share to smaller, more efficient plants, which, in turn, increase their employment.

All sectors reduce energy consumption in response to higher energy prices

Allowing for heterogeneous effects at the sector level shows that plants in almost every sector reduce their energy use in response to higher energy prices (Figure 9.2). The main equation above is estimated for each two-digit sector separately, allowing to investigate whether plants in different sectors react differently to changes in energy costs. The coefficient estimates are displayed in Figure 9.2, showing that almost all sectors reduce their energy use significantly, especially the largest sectors (with the exception of the food industry). This finding also applies to total CO_2 emissions.

Figure 9.2. Changes in energy use by sector

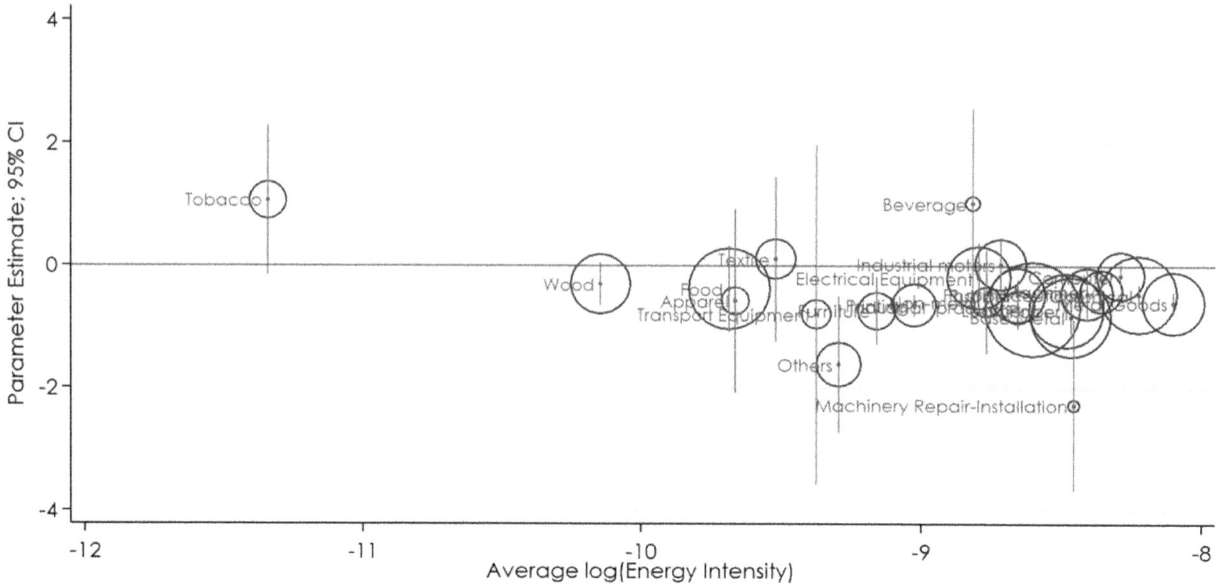

Note: The figure presents the parameter estimates from sector-specific regressions. Each point is weighted by the sum of total output to reflect the relative size of the sector, illustrated by the circles.
Source: Brucal and Dechezleprêtre (2021[1]).

No significant employment effects found at the industry-level

The industry-level analysis shows no statistically significant effects on job destruction, job creation, or net employment in response to rising energy prices (see Brucal and Dechezleprêtre (2021[1]), for estimation results). Consistent with the previous findings from the within-sector estimation, where only small plants were found to slightly increase their employment, results at the industry-level show no effects on net job creation.

Conclusion

Rising energy prices in the Indonesian manufacturing sector reduced emissions significantly without large negative effects on economic outcomes

The results of the study show that energy price increases in the Indonesian manufacturing industry led to significant reductions in energy use and thus CO_2 emissions, while large economic effects were absent. A 10% increase in energy prices is found to reduce CO_2 emissions by 5.8% on average, while employment is reduced by 0.2%. There are no other negative economic effects found, i.e. on real output. The CO_2 reduction combined with a constant output implies a decrease in energy-intensity of output, which is found to be driven by updates in the capital stock of plants. The effects are found to be heterogeneous across plants, depending on their initial output, energy-intensity, and sector they operate in. Larger plants as well as more energy-intensive plants are found to decrease their energy use more. For the economic outcomes, smaller plants are found to increase their employment with rising energy prices, while larger plants do not react to changes in energy prices. For all plants, rising energy prices increase the probability of plant exit. However, at the aggregate sectoral level, no significant employment effects are detected, suggesting that job losses due to plant exit are compensated by increases in the employment in surviving plants.

The effects on demand for skilled and unskilled labour are not accounted for in analysis

The results of the analysis suggest that surviving plants adopt newer and energy-saving technologies. It remains, however, outside of the scope of this study, how this change in technologies affects the demand for skilled and unskilled labour – and thus potentially the wage distribution. The study is thus not able to analyse whether energy subsidy reforms do, as they are often assumed to, harm the poorest citizens most through changes in demand for unskilled labour.

Economic effects of rising energy prices might be lower in emerging economies due to more flexible labour markets

Energy subsidy reforms are shown to have significant positive effects in terms of environmental outcomes while almost having no effects in terms of economic outcomes. Reallocation effects in terms of employment are found to be small without effects at the industry level. Comparing this analysis to the analysis summarised in the previous chapter, suggests that economic effects of rising energy prices might be lower in emerging economies. One reason for this might be that emerging economies have more flexible labour markets, which allows firms to adapt more quickly and more flexibly to new environmental policy settings.

Notes

[1] The chapter is a summary of "Assessing the impact of energy prices on plant-level environmental and economic performance: Evidence from Indonesian manufacturers" (2021[1]) by A. Brucal and A. Dechezleprêtre, OECD Environment Working Papers, No. 170, OECD Publishing, Paris.

References

Al-Sahlawi, M. (1989), "The demand for natural gas: a survey of price and income elasticities", *The Energy Journal*, Vol. 10/1, pp. 77-90, https://www.jstor.org/stable/41322309. [7]

Bohi, D. and M. Zimmerman (1984), "An update on econometric studies of energy demand behavior", *Annual Review of Energy*, Vol. 9/1, pp. 105-154, https://doi.org/10.1146/annurev.eg.09.110184.000541. [6]

Brons, M. et al. (2008), "A meta-analysis of the price elasticity of gasoline demand. A SUR approach", *Energy Economics*, Vol. 30/5, pp. 2105-2122, https://doi.org/10.1016/j.eneco.2007.08.004. [9]

Brucal, A. and A. Dechezleprêtre (2021), "Assessing the impact of energy prices on plant-level environmental and economic performance: Evidence from Indonesian manufacturers", *OECD Environment Working Paper No. 170*, https://doi.org/10.1787/9ec54222-en. [1]

Cole, M., R. Elliot and L. Zhang (2017), "Foreign direct investment and the environment", *Annual Review of Environmental and Resources*, Vol. 42, pp. 465-487, https://doi.org/10.1146/annurev-environ-102016-060916. [3]

Davis, S. and J. Haltiwanger (1992), "Gross job creation, gross job destruction, and employment reallocation", *The Quarterly Journal of Economics*, Vol. 107/3, pp. 819-863, https://www.jstor.org/stable/2118365. [15]

Dussaux, D. (2020), "The joint effects of energy prices and carbon taxes on environmental and economic performance: Evidence from the French manufacturing sector", *OECD Environment Working Papers*, No. 154, OECD Publishing, Paris, https://dx.doi.org/10.1787/b84b1b7d-en. [12]

Espey, M. (1996), "Explaining the variation in elasticity estimates for gasoline demand in the United States: a meta-analysis", *The Energy Journal*, Vol. 17/3, pp. 49-60, https://www.jstor.org/stable/41322693. [8]

Havranek, T., Z. Irsova and K. Janda (2012), "Demand for gasoline is more price-inelastic than commonly thought", *Energy Economics*, Vol. 34/1, pp. 201-207, https://doi.org/10.1016/j.eneco.2011.09.003. [10]

Houthakker, H. (1951), "Some calculations on electricity consumption in Great Britain", *Journal of the Royal Statistical Society*, Vol. 114/3, pp. 359-371, https://www.jstor.org/stable/2980781. [4]

Labandeira, X., J. Labeaga and X. Lopez-Otero (2017), "A meta-analysis on the price elasticity of energy demand", *Energy Policy*, Vol. 102, pp. 549-568, https://doi.org/10.1016/j.enpol.2017.01.002. [11]

Marin, G. and F. Vona (2017), "The impact of energy prices on employment and environmental performance: Evidence from French manufacturing establishments", *Working Paper 053.2017, Fondazione Eni Enrico Mattei*, https://www.ofce.sciences-po.fr/pdf/dtravail/WP2017-26.pdf. [13]

Rentschler, J. and M. Kornejew (2017), "Energy price variation and competitiveness: Firm level evidence from Indonesia", *Energy Economics*, Vol. 67/C, pp. 242-254, https://doi.org/10.1016/j.eneco.2017.08.015. [2]

Sato, M. et al. (2019), "International and sectoral variation in industry energy prices 1995-2015", *Energy Economics*, Vol. 78, pp. 235-258. [14]

Taylor, L. (1975), "The demand for electricity: a survey", *The Bell Journal of Economics*, Vol. 6/1, pp. 74-110, https://www.jstor.org/stable/pdf/3003216.pdf. [5]

www.ingramcontent.com/pod-product-compliance
Ingram Content Group UK Ltd.
Pitfield, Milton Keynes, MK11 3LW, UK
UKHW051506290926
15471UKWH00008B/1453